Connecting Latitudes

~

On Land and Sea

Barbara J. Euser

Copyright © 2021 by Barbara J. Euser
All rights reserved

For permission to reprint essays, please contact
the author at bjeuser@yahoo.com

Published by
Writers' Workshops International
3465 County Road 23
Fort Lupton, Colorado 80621
United States of America

Library of Congress Control Number: 2020926002

Cataloging Data

Sailing—Offshore
Canal boating—France
Mountaineering—Russia
Cross-country skiing
Running—Zagreb marathon
Traveling with children—India
Trekking—Nepal
Trekking—China
Bosnia—Elections
Croatia—Zagreb marathon
Colombia
Italy
Ireland
Greece

ISBN: 978-0-9842992-4-9

Interior Design by Dianne Nelson
Cover Design by Adam Phillips

Printed in the United States of America

Contents

~

CHAPTER ONE: MOUNTAINS

Unanticipated Snow Cave 2
Descent from Mount Communism 11
Trekking with the Tiger 19
Orphans on Top of the World 29

CHAPTER TWO: POLITICAL CONSIDERATIONS

Reflections on Burning a Cocaine Lab. 34
Helping with Bosnian Elections 40
Running the Zagreb Marathon. 51

CHAPTER THREE: ON BOARD

Across the Sea 58
Sailing the Singlehanded TransPac 73
Lurley and the Singlehanded TransPac 88
Chez Paul. 98

~ CONTENTS ~

CHAPTER FOUR: INDIA, IRELAND AND ITALY

Kerala with Two Girls in Tow 103
Winegeese 113
Pangur Bán. 121
Mussel Farming in Taranto. 127
Magna Graecia. 134

CHAPTER FIVE: GREECE

Vines of Vatika. 143
Pathway to Paradise. 151
Cultivating Olives 157
Turtle Tracks 164
Eternal Pavlopetri 171

Story Sources. 180

About the Author 183

*To my daughters Laney and Piper,
who are connecting latitudes in their own lives*

Introduction

~

Over the years, my travel essays have appeared in magazines and anthologies. I have collected some of my favorites here. Criss-crossing continents and latitudes, settings range from Steamboat Springs, Colorado, to Mount Communism in Russia, across the Atlantic Ocean, and as far as Kauai, Hawaii, in the Pacific. Dates range from 1971 to 2020.

This collection of travel essays has been in the back of my mind for years. But I was always too busy, too engaged pursuing new activities, to find the time I needed to pull together a book. The 2020 pandemic ground activities to a halt. In Greece, the government imposed a lock-down, loosened it, then imposed it again. During this period of imposed lock-down, I finally found the cushion of time I needed to search through old files, dig out paper clippings from magazines, and organize them into a more-or-less logical sequence.

Each one of the places I have written about is close to my heart. The places in Greece, I visit every day. Other places,

~ INTRODUCTION ~

I know I will not visit again. That brings a sense of loss, but also a sense of gratitude—thanks that I experienced these things I am now sharing with you.

—Barbara J. Euser
January 2021
Neapolis, Greece

~

CHAPTER ONE

~

Mountains

Unanticipated Snow Cave

~

The powder plumed lightly as I telemarked down the off-piste back bowls of Steamboat Springs ski area. The sky was a brilliant Colorado blue. Wispy clouds floated high overhead. A good four hours of skiing essentially downhill through fresh powder, followed by dinner with a friend—hard physical activity outdoors plus the promise of good food and good conversation was my idea of a perfect day!

I had slept in that morning after working late the night before. It was noon before I took the first lift up to the top of the ski area. A late start—but it had only taken about four hours to do this route the one time I had done it before. Ski bumming for the season, I skied either downhill or cross-country for a few hours almost every day. People's schedules were unpredictable. Sometimes I'd hook up with someone on the mountain, sometimes not. But I wasn't looking for company that day; it wasn't going to be a leisurely social afternoon. I wanted to ski hard for a few hours, take advantage of the beautiful day, then get cleaned up for a date I was looking forward to.

One short, narrow section of my route concerned me. It was a drop-off right above a waterfall. Before, my friends and I had helped each other over the potentially dangerous

~ *Mountains* ~

spot. Each person would station himself at the bottom of the drop-off, offer a hand, and spot the next person coming down. That way the skier coming down couldn't slip over the lip of the stream bank into the water. I began to worry about how I would get past that section skiing alone. I figured I could go very slowly, and if it looked too hard to manage on my own, I would find another route through the trees.

The deep powder that was so lovely to ski down on the steeper slopes stopped me as the slopes flattened out. Breaking trail slowed me. What had started out as a four-hour afternoon jaunt was turning out quite differently. Before I had even made it to the drop off, the sun had slipped below the mountaintops. As it began to get dark, I considered my options. Far below, I could see a dirt road. I was in a drainage that looked as though it connected directly with the road. The unknown route looked simpler than the route I knew. I guessed it involved more distance, but it looked like less aggravation. Trying out an unknown route this late in the day was clearly risky. I was tired and the danger of the drop-off loomed larger and larger. I convinced myself the unknown risk was less than the one knew.

Darkness settled over the mountain. I realized I would be late for dinner and wondered whether my friend would think I had stood him up. I would just have to explain. It was taking much longer than I thought to go the "direct" way back to civilization. A side creek interrupted my descent. I would have to contour around it.

The slope was getting steep and I didn't want to lose any more elevation. I started a kick turn. I lifted my right ski up and flipped the toe to the right. I then put the ski down and transferred my weight. But as I leaned forward, putting my full weight on the ski, the ski wasn't there. I fell forward on my face and started sliding head first down the steep slope. My left ski was still attached and to my boot and flopped back and forth as I skidded helplessly downward. My poles dangled uselessly as I tried to stop myself with my arms. My mouth filled with snow. I felt as if I were drowning.

It may have been snow accumulating in front of me that finally stopped my fall. I don't know. When I was able to breathe again, I tried to stand up, but only floundered in the deep fresh powder. I had one ski and one remaining pole; I lost one pole during my fall. I didn't know whether or not my right ski had slid down the slope ahead of me. Looking down at the creek below, I realized how lucky I was to have stopped where I did. Another few seconds and I could have slid right into a "hole" in the creek—a spot the snow doesn't cover—and into the fast-flowing water.

My situation was not very good. It was dark. I had only one ski. The snow was too deep for me to make any progress at all walking—I would sink to my hips with every step. I couldn't go anywhere. One the other hand, I hadn't broken any bones. I was physically intact. I did have a daypack with a few items in it. And I was right at the base of a tree. There was no point in floundering through the deep snow. How far would I get? With a sense of despair, I realized the best thing to do was to burrow into the snow for the night.

On the slope just above the trunk of the tree, I dug into the snow. Alternately digging and flattening the snow to create a cave that would not collapse, I fashioned a space just large enough to curl up in. I left as much of an overhang of snow as possible for insulation against the cold, clear night. I enjoy winter camping—but my previous experience had included a tent and sleeping bag. For fun, one afternoon I had built a snow cave with friends and we had sat inside with a stove and made tea. Building a snow cave for survival was something I had only read about.

Very carefully, I squeezed my five feet seven inches into the tiny snow cave. The digging, and before that the skiing, had kept me warm. But now I started to get cold. Positioned in my frozen nest, I wondered how I would get through the night. I pulled my old down jacket out of my daypack and struggled into it. I worried about my toes. My cross-country ski boots were leather, but not very well insulated and a little tight. I took off my boots and stuffed my feet and boots into the daypack. The pack fabric provided a layer of insulation up to my calves. When I had set out for my afternoon ski, as a nod to emergency preparedness, I included a stub of candle, a few matches, and a couple of small Hershey bars in my pack. At the University of Colorado, I was a member of the Rocky Mountain Rescue Group. We spent hours reviewing what hikers and climbers had done wrong, thus creating emergency situations. Then we discussed what they should have done before we had to go out and search for them or pull them off the mountain. Here I wore both hats. I created the emergency by going skiing alone in the afternoon, then compounded it by deciding to try an unknown route. I was also my only rescuer, relying on what I had learned vicariously from others' errors. It was going to be a miserable night.

I stared at the walls of my tiny cave thinking. I had on a wool hat and gloves with waterproof shells, a down jacket, and wool socks. Not too bad. But I seriously regretted wearing jeans without long underwear for my afternoon ski. I silently resolved never to make that mistake again. I thought about all the things I wished I had: a flashlight, something made of wool for my legs, a space blanket, food, a stove. My body was cooling down. I pulled my single long, brown braid around my neck, hoping for some protection.

I decided to light the candle. It might not provide much warmth, but it would at least create an illusion of warmth. I felt a flicker of pride in my strike-anywhere matches kept dry in a film canister. Too bad there were only six of them. And there weren't many places to strike them. Happily, my jeans had a metal zipper. I thought of Jack London's story. Would the roof of my mini-cave collapse if I lit the candle? I would shield the snow with my hands, collecting every bit of warmth I could. Damned if I would let the snow have any precious heat. The first match fizzled. The second match lit and I touched it to the wick. Just the sight of the tiny flame warmed me. The light changed the character of the snow cave and made it almost inviting. I nearly burned the palm of my hand as I cupped the flame. I consulted my watch. How could it be only eight o'clock?

The candle burned down quickly. I curled my fingers as close as I could to the flame, absorbing every calorie of energy. Whatever I did, I had to protect my long, piano-playing fingers. When the candle was half gone, I decided I would take the chance of being able to light it again. I snuffed it out with my fingers.

Part of surviving the night would be keeping myself awake and amused as much as possible. In the light, I had rationed my two Hershey bars. I decided to eat them two squares at a time. In the dark again, I ate my first candy treat. Without candlelight, I couldn't tell how much time passed. I allowed myself another ration of chocolate, then another. Surely hours had gone by. Time to light the candle again.

Carefully I struck the match on my zipper. Again the first match fizzled. I groaned. The second match caught. The cave was again transformed into near-cheeriness. But it was only nine-thirty. How could time pass so slowly? How could I endure an entire night of minutes that took hours to go by?

Again the candle burned quickly. I decided to burn it completely and not take a chance on lighting it successfully a third time. As before, I trapped every flicker of its warmth. Too soon, it sputtered out in the snow. I faced the rest of the night in unrelieved darkness.

Waiting as long as I could between servings, I savored each remaining square of chocolate. Finally, they too were gone. I was exhausted and colder than I had ever been in my twenty-one years. I knew I should try to stay awake. I remembered the tale of the little match girl and every other story I had heard about people falling asleep and freezing to death. I wondered how long it would take my friends to miss me. I wondered if my stood-up date would be worried, or just mad at me. Would my housemates recognize that I was gone, or assume that I was with my friend? I wasn't supposed to be at my job cooking Mexican food at El Rancho Restaurant again until the following evening. Via mental telepathy, I sent a personalized call for help to everyone I could think of. Finally, I couldn't keep myself awake any longer. I fell asleep shivering.

While unconscious, my soul drifted away. Instantly I understood the old spiritual, "Let Me Fly"—I was indeed flying. Flying at an extraordinarily high speed. My soul was released from my body. I could see myself lying in the little makeshift snow cave at the base of the spruce tree. I felt very sad that my parents, relatives, and friends would think I had died. They would mistake that flesh for me. Illuminated, I understood why even our miraculous bodies may be referred to as "lumps of clay." They are clay in contrast to the lightness of our souls. My soul was speeding away from its earthbound existence. I was completely happy and relieved to be released. My only regret was that people would not understand. A universe of possibilities was opening up as I raced through the darkness like a speeding star. I hadn't thought of my body as a restraint, but once freed, I recognized how confining it had been. As I sped on, I also understood that I would not turn back. The idea of spirits returning to the world made no sense. There was no way to leave a message for relatives or friends that I was happier and freer than I had ever been. Thoughts were short-circuited and came to me as flashes of understanding. There were too many levels of opportunity stretching out in front of me to waste time worrying about an earlier, inferior form of existence.

I woke up with my thigh muscles in convulsions. My whole body shook. I had been perfectly happy being released, and here I was back in my miserable cold body. I had been granted only a preview this time. For the rest of the night, I shivered, awake, in my cave.

As soon as the sky lightened, I unfolded myself, dug my boots out of my daypack, and struggled to put them on my feet. I was not thinking clearly, but I knew I had to start moving and climb back up the hill. Slowly, painstakingly, I worked my way up. I laid my ski across the snow, using it as a platform for my arms, while I stomped steps for my feet in the powdery fluff. As soon as I took one step up, I moved the ski and repeated the effort. My blood started circulating and I wasn't freezing any more.

Halfway up the slope, I picked up the lost pole. Finally, I reached the spot where I had fallen. My right ski was there in the snow, ready for me to put weight on it. Forcing my fingers to fasten the bindings, I put my skis on again. Which way to go? I was afraid to continue down the drainage because other side creeks might deter me. I was also afraid to contour around the mountain and pass the narrow section I had dreaded the night before. Hungry, moving very slowly, I retraced my tracks of the day before.

I skied uphill all day. About four in the afternoon, I crossed the rope barrier into the ski area. The lifts had closed and a snow cat was grooming the slopes. I waved my arms frantically until the driver noticed me. By radio, he informed the area office that the lost cross-country skier had been found.

That evening I learned that my friends had indeed worried and informed the sheriff's office that I had gone cross-country skiing and had not returned. When my date had shown up to take me to dinner, they realized my cross-country skies were gone. A helicopter had crisscrossed the area in the morning, but had not seen me struggling in the trees. Two friends had followed my tracks, but when they saw the tracks heading down the drainage, decided I had skied out on my own. That my friends had sounded an alarm, then taken their day to ski after me, made me feel deeply grateful and, at the same time, exceedingly embarrassed that I had put myself in such a situation.

The entire experience—from a fabulous afternoon of cross-country skiing to shivering near death in a snow cave—lasted only thirty hours. I am thankful for the fleeting preview of death, more determined than ever to be mindful of life.

Descent From Mount Communism

~

Five climbers trudged across the 20,000-foot-high plateau dragging a long object wrapped in a nylon tent. With each step, they sank thigh-deep in the recent snow. Wrapped inside the tent was a sixth member of the climbing team. She had fallen into a deep coma two days earlier. The only way to get her off the mountain was to drag her along in a makeshift sled.

    I remember the fall a couple of days earlier. In the morning, we had come across three members of a German climbing team that had been stranded on the side of Mt. Communism at about 22,000 feet. (At 24,500 feet, Mount Communism is the highest peak in the former Soviet Union.) The four members of our team who had made it as high as 23,800 feet were retreating. Three days earlier, an avalanche had swept away three members of another team camped above us. Our tent had collapsed in the accumulating snow, despite our repeated attempts to dig it out. The time allotted to us to reach the summit of Mt. Communism had run out. In the strictly controlled climbing environment, we had agreed to make our final summit attempt by a specific date. When the weather didn't cooperate, we were required to descend. Two members of an Austrian team had camped near us and turned back the same day we did. On the descent, we all spent one night at our previous campsite at 23,000 feet.

Descending in a white-out the next morning, we came across an abandoned-looking tent. The three Germans inside were in bad shape. We had heard them on our radio days earlier calling for assistance. But because of the storm, no one had been able to reach them. They were badly dehydrated and unable to walk steadily. As we helped them get ready to join us in the descent, we realized they had lost their fine motor skills. They were unable to put on their own crampons. They were letting their gloves blow away in the gusting wind. We buckled their crampons, dressed them in their hats and gloves, handed them their ice axes. Then we roped them together so they could descend in parallel to us. That was too much for them to accomplish. They couldn't walk together. One of them kept falling down and the other two were too weak to assist him. The two Austrians left our rope to climb down by themselves. We added the three Germans to our rope.

The blowing snow was so thick we could not see where we were heading. The climb up had not been extremely steep, just tediously uphill. However, as we headed down to the camp on the 20,000-foot-high plateau below us, we blindly veered onto steeper and steeper terrain. I was the last person on the rope. My friend Jini was just ahead of me. All at once, the rope connecting us jerked tight and I was pulled off balance. Jini was already sliding down, flipping over into arrest position, jamming her ice axe into the snow. As soon as I started falling, I did the same. The full weight of my body and the heavy pack on my back were forcing my ice axe into the snow, willing it to hold us, willing us to stop sliding. Then I was plucked backwards off the snow, flying downward through the air, until I hit the snow, sliding down head first on my back, ice axe still clutched in my gloves.

The seven of us were in a snow slide—perhaps in falling we had fractured the fresh, unstable powder. I realized the snow and climbers were sliding down the mountain together, then all of a sudden, I stopped moving. Like an anchor, the snow had caught me fast. All the others on the rope were arrested in sequence, like dolls on a long rubber band. It took a moment for me to realize I could still breathe. My face was up, covered with only a light layer of snow. I couldn't move, my arms pinned in the snow by the straps of my backpack. Gratefully, I sucked in air. After the initial relief, I began struggling to free my arms. Gradually, I worked my shoulders out of the pack straps and my arms followed to the surface. At that moment, the leader of our rope reached me. He told me all the others were safe, regrouping after our fall. One colleague had been suspended in the air over a small cliff when the rope jerked taut. With careful maneuvering, the others had eased him down. Slowly, we assembled our gear and our selves. From where our fall ended, it was only an hour's hike down to our previous campsite on the plateau.

We reached the plateau, unroped and walked along together, chatting and joking in the aftermath of near disaster. Then I fell over. Momentarily, I had lost consciousness. Someone called, "Hey, get up!" and dazedly, I did. When asked what had happened I couldn't say. I knew I hadn't tripped over my crampon or fallen for any obvious reason. Mystified, I walked on slowly. Putting up the tent that evening seemed like a terrible effort and I sat to the side, watching my climbing partners do the work. I had no excuse, I just couldn't make myself participate. After a dinner of freeze-dried stew, we crawled into our sleeping bags. It was days before someone pulled me out of mine.

Jini, my closest friend on the expedition, told me the next part of this story, about the days I can't remember.

The next morning after our fall, I didn't get out of bed in the morning, despite the exhortations of my partners. Finally, they realized I wasn't asleep, but unconscious. The four members of our team, plus two who had descended from our 23,000-foot camp because one was experiencing symptoms of pulmonary edema, were at one end of the 20,000-foot-high plateau, a prominent feature of Mt. Communism. It was six miles across the plateau to the other end, which was another day's climb along a rock ridge and down a steep slope to a camp at 16,000 feet. Then there was one more day's hike across a serrated glacier to a base camp at 13,000 feet.

My unconscious condition presented a serious problem to my partners. The day before we had been involved in a serious fall because we were trying to accommodate members of another climbing party who were not able to descend by themselves. With the descent to lower altitude and plenty of fluids, their condition had improved and they were able to continue on their own. However, now I was a serious liability to my partners. The doctor who was with us was only able to say that other than being unconscious, I was in apparently good condition. He couldn't conjecture about whether I was suffering brain damage in connection to being in a coma. However, the longer I stayed in a coma, the more likely brain damage would be.

During the series of storms that had buffeted the mountain while we were making our way toward the summit, several feet of snow had fallen on the plateau. It was beginning to consolidate, but breaking trail was an arduous task. Every footstep meant sinking to one's thighs. In planning for the expedition, we had carefully included backpackers' snowshoes in our gear, but when we initially arrived on the plateau, it was hard-packed glacier ice. There seemed no good reason to carry snowshoes on our backs all the way to the other end of the plateau just to carry them back again. It was a decision much regretted over the next couple of days.

My colleagues determined to drag me off the mountain. There is no alternative in a situation like that: a climbing team has to depend on its own ingenuity. They wrapped the tent around me like a colorful cocoon and took a photograph. Then they started dragging me through the hip-deep snow. It took two days to go six miles. No one was sure whether they were dragging a person or a vegetable. But they didn't consider abandoning their burden.

That night, I showed a sign of consciousness. Some event during the day had caused a disagreement and it continued in the tent after supper. I had been placed, still in my sleeping bag between two of my partners in an attempt to keep me as warm as possible. The argument got more and more heated. My partners were yelling at each other. Suddenly, I sat up in my sleeping bag and shouted "Stop it now!" Then I slumped back down. I vaguely remember being irritated enough, even in my unconscious state, to want to make them stop.

Once they arrived with their package at the beginning of the plateau, they faced a bigger challenge. The rock ridge we had traversed to arrive at the plateau was narrow and exposed. There was no way to drag a body along it. They decided to put me in a backpack and carry me. They emptied my pack and cut holes in the bottom corners for my legs to stick out. Several days before, the strongest member of our team had gone all the way down to the base camp at 13,000 feet with another member who was showing signs of pulmonary edema. We were in touch with the base camp every day by radio. Steve had been summoned back up to the plateau to help with my evacuation. Somehow, my colleagues stuffed me into my backpack, but the painful position brought me to semi-consciousness. I have a vivid impression of Steve staggering under my essentially dead weight on his back. I was too heavy for him. He couldn't hope to negotiate the delicate ridge while barely able to maintain himself upright. I remember the view, looking over his shoulder down from the plateau on blue and white plains below.

There was a team of Russian climbers about to begin their descent of the ridge. My team members appealed to them for help. Someone volunteered. Again, I was hoisted onto a man's back. The backpack hurt my legs and I remember the impression of patterned mitten-backs. The design seemed to me like the totem pole designs of the Indians of the Pacific Northwest. Then as my savior carefully inched his way along the ridge, holding onto the rock pinnacles with his hands as we passed along the edge of the cliffs below, I had the impression that we were working our way around the perimeter of a stone cathedral. Those moments of semi-consciousness were brief and I'm not sure anyone remarked on them. But they are all I have of four days' time.

Jini told me that the next section of the descent also affected me, though I do not remember. The steep climb up the snow had been accomplished on fixed ropes traversing the slope. There was no way to drag me down, and there was no need for the person who had managed to carry me along the ridge to risk himself further. Wrapped in the tent once again, my colleagues lowered me on ropes to the base of the slope. As they belayed me down, I began to travel faster and faster. Finally, I sat up and screamed. Amazed, my belayers stopped me and resumed at a slower pace. On the fourth day, my climbing partners faced a glacier melted into icy points. There was no way to drag me across the uneven surface. A stretcher was brought from the base camp and my colleagues and other volunteers took turns negotiating the difficult terrain without dumping me.

That night I dreamed I had malaria. I thought I was sweating in my sleeping bag. It was wet and sticky. I was beginning to come to and I was peeing for the first time in days.

The next day, at the 13,000-foot base camp, I was examined by all the medical personnel at the camp. Discussions went on at length. People crowded around the cot where I was lying. I could see and hear them, but I couldn't move. Someone pinned a brass bear to the collar of my shirt. From the discussion in Russian, which I do not speak, I go the impression that there was some special connection between us. Perhaps he was the person who carried me across the rock ridge.

I was taken by helicopter directly to the city of Osh, bypassing the helicopter ride to the basecamp at 11,000 feet and the day-long bus ride between there and Osh. I was put in the hospital. Still unable to move, I watched and listened to the nurses discussing me in sympathetic tones. They fingered my long hair and talked about whether it was so matted that it should just be cut off. Instead, a nurse on night duty decided to try to untangle it. She sat patiently beside me for hours, combing the knots out of my hair. The doctor on our climbing team insisted that I not receive any medical treatment at the hospital in Osh. The hospital facilities made me think of something from a 1930's movie. The nursing care was excellent, however, and I regained a bit of muscular control. After a couple of days, I stood up and took a few unsteady steps. My climbing partners called me "Lurch." It was a great relief to be able to joke about it.

Despite various tests I took over the ensuing months, no one could say what caused me to lapse into a coma. Perhaps my brain swelled after hitting against my skull when I acted as an anchor during our fall down the mountain. Or perhaps I suffered from high-altitude cerebral edema. I will never know for certain. For some reason, I recovered completely from four days of unconsciousness at 20,000 feet elevation. I ask myself why. I am filled with a sense that I have a debt to repay. I cannot pay it directly, but such debts are rarely paid to whomever or whatever they are owed. The debt for the years that were added to my life through no effort of my own is enormous. Repayment will take the rest of my life—and all my creative efforts.

Trekking with the Tiger

~

There is a Chinese saying, "It is easier to get to Heaven than to Yunnan." It is indeed a long and difficult journey to Yunnan to explore one of the deepest canyons in the world—Tiger Leaping Gorge. That is part of its allure.

The Chang Jiang or Long River, which we know as the Yangtze, flows through many gorges on its way across China to the Pacific Ocean, but none as deep or dramatic as Tiger Leaping Gorge. Deeper than the Grand Canyon, the wide Yangtze valley narrows into a vertical chasm 7,000 feet deep, over twenty miles long, not separated into wide rims, but falling almost straight down.

Philosophically it is also difficult to make the decision to even travel to China in the face of the tragedy that took place four years ago in Tiananmen Square in June 1989. The same government that was in power then remains. But contact with Westerners is vitally important to Chinese citizens who are interested in learning what Western people and politics are all about. Thus, my fellow traveler Rick and I rationalized our decision to travel to China and, as part of our journey, hike through Tiger Leaping Gorge.

Physically, the journey itself is demanding: first flying to the bicycle-thronged megalopolis of Shanghai, followed by a second flight from there to Chengdu, the capital of Sichuan Province, the agricultural breadbasket of China; from Chengdu, via an overnight train with hard benches to stretch out a maybe sleep on—known as a hard sleeper—to Dukou, a saga in itself; from Dukou, a thirteen-hour bus ride to Lijiang on dirt roads over major mountain passes; from the medium-sized city of Lijiang a three-hour bus ride to the smaller city of Baihanchang. Once we arrived in Baihanchang, we had to seek out our own transportation.

Carrying out backpacks, we left the main route and heading toward Qiaotou, the town closest to the gorge. Amid the well-groomed farms of the Yangtze River valley, rickety country busses are few and far between. Sitting on a wooden plank between the roots of an ancient tree, we jumped up and waved at each canvas-covered lorry as it passed. Empty or full of furniture or pigs, none would stop. Finally, as dusk crept in, a walking tractor—a diesel engine with a seat pulling a metal wagon—came by. The middle-aged driver in his blue Mao suit dropped his passengers off. We offered him twenty-five yuan for a ride to Qiaotou, but he insisted on fifty yuan, about ten U.S. dollars. That seemed an exorbitant amount considering a bus ticket cost eight yuan. But we had seen no busses, the lorry drivers would not have us, and it would be dark soon.

Having charged a first-class price, our driver was determined to provide a first-class ride. He offered cigarettes, but neither Rick nor I smoke. Then, from farmers selling fruit by the side of the road, our driver bought us Asian pears. As we coasted down through the Yangtze valley, the evening sun filtered through the tassels of corn plants in fields lining the powerful Yangtze. We crunched our sweet, grainy fruit. The mud-red river shone as the sun slipped behind the ridge 3,000 feet above.

After an hour and a half, a nineteenth-century stone bridge across the Yangtze loomed, the last before the gorge. As our driver started across the bridge, two bridge guardians—seventy-year-old men dressed in People's Liberation Army uniforms, one with a rifle—motioned our driver to stop. "Foreigners are not allowed to cross the bridge," the bridge guards insisted. Despite our explanation that we were going to Tiger Leaping Gorge, an open area, and had been there before (at least Rick had been near the gorge), the taller guard went into his kiosk and pulled out a bi-lingual book of regulations. He found the one with the English translation: "Foreigners are not allowed to enter this area." We showed the guard our passports and previous Chinese visas to demonstrate that we were *lao pengyou*—old friends—of China. After a considerable discussion, carried out mostly with our hands and a few basic Chinese phrases, the guard changed his mind and let us pass.

The next morning, traveling the last mile from Qiaotou to the gorge, again sitting on our backpacks in the trailer of a walking tractor, we passed the official entrance. It is marked by a marble statue of a plump, friendly-looking tiger running toward the edge of the gorge. The legend is that the tiger, running away from a hunter, leapt across the gorge to make his escape. At the narrowest section of the gorge—a mere thirty feet across—one imagines it might have been possible.

At the gorge entrance, the road ends. A building under construction is intended to become a tourist hotel. A road all the way through the gorge to Daqu, the small town on the other side of the river at the lower end of the gorge, is to be completed in three years. Dozens of workers chipped stones and moved rubble by hand; the three-year estimate seemed overly-ambitious. In its constant effort to attract foreign currency, China is changing the character of its natural wonders, including Tiger Leaping Gorge, by developing them to appeal to tourists who want to stay in high-quality hotels and expect Western-style amenities. It is planned that what is now a remote canyon, accessible only on foot, will become a Mecca to be viewed from the comfort of an air-conditioned bus.

Rick and I wanted to experience the gorge on foot, before its character had been changed. In the never-ending debate between leaving some places accessible to only a hardy few, versus opening up wonders for everyone to see, I vote for access by the hardy few. There are places so remote in this world, I will never have the opportunity to see them—and that is a good thing. Some places must remain wild.

Tiger Leaping Gorge is not wilderness. The gorge is sparsely populated by farmers whose high-angle fields are located high above the footpath that connects them to the rest of the world. These tiny farms cling to the steep hillsides, farmers eking out a subsistence living. Though not pristine, the Gorge is far from developed.

Past the end of the construction, the dirt trail becomes a single-track footpath leading up and down over landslides, clinging precariously to the sides of the cliffs, as the Yangtze River rushes ever downwards. A mile within the gorge, the upper falls create a quarter-mile-long furious cauldron. The river plunges down and curls back on itself in the holes beneath the huge, rounded boulders. Despite attempts, no one has yet run the length of Tiger Leaping Gorge by boat. The river rushes down the gorge, but the trail, etched in the cliffside, heads up. Black, oxidized limestone cliffs and five- thousand- to six-thousand-foot-high ridges and peaks rise along the opposite side of the gorge. On our side of the gorge, half-a-dozen spectacular waterfalls, hundreds of feet high, run down side canyons and across the trail.

A fellow hiker joined us. He was a Naxi trader who bought jade and jewelry in Lhasa, then took them to Guilin to sell to tourists. Of course, since Tiananmen, Western tourists were less common, but Taiwanese tourists were more abundant, and they in particular like the old jade from Tibet, the trader said.

We had hired a horse, guided by its owner, to carry out packs. After a little more than one hour, we came to another waterfall crossing the trail, plunging hundreds of feet down before its final drop into the Yangtze. The pathway crossing was nicely-leveled stonework, but narrow. It did not appear especially hazardous. But as the young horse owner led his horse out into the water, the inside pack caught on the bank. Taking one sideways step, the horse's back leg thrashed into the air over the edge of the three-hundred-foot waterfall. Desperately, we tried to loosen the load. Finally, we managed to drag the packs back along the path. With nothing on its back, the horse regained its footing and gingerly picked its way across the waterfall. We had salvaged the situation. But the young horse owner's confidence was shaken. He could have lost his most prized possession, his greatest asset, because of one mis-step. He was unwilling to take any more risks. Horse packing for the afternoon was over. We paid the young owner and he and his horse headed back toward Qiaotou.

Rick and I shouldered our packs and hiked along the trail, the Yangtze River crashing through the gorge below. The trail was narrow and there was nowhere to comfortably stop. By late afternoon, we found a flat spot where we could pitch our tent. While we were staking the rain fly, an old Chinese farmer in faded clothes walked by. He pointed to the overhang above us. "*Wanshang xiayu*—evening rain falls," he said,"*Shitou xialai*—rocks come down." We reviewed our situation. The man had given us fair warning. The nylon tent would withstand rain, not rocks. We were exhausted from the emotions of the near-accident and a day of hiking up the trail. Reluctantly, we decided to take down the tent and re-pitch it.

The sky cleared a bit and the sun came through—just enough to turn the clouds drifting in the peaks across the gorge a pale peach. We sat on the edge of the trail, watching the sun set: the fading light reflected and clouds glowed, while the river rushed endlessly below. Then it started to rain and continued heavily through the night.

Morning was completely gray. Clouds laced their fingers through the ridges of the canyon. A few steps from the tent, cradling steaming cups of tea in our hands, we looked up the length of the gorge. The brown river churned, carrying seventy-five thousand cubic feet of water per second to the sea. From where we stood, Tiger Leaping Gorge appeared to have three distinct levels: a pale set of cliffs rising directly from the water, a second set of diamond-shaped faces, vertical cliffs of black, oxidized limestone, and a third level of spires and towers, deeply eroded into majestic forms. Above the spires, hidden by the clouds, were the peaks. We caught glimpses of the highest summits through the clouds, but never gained a clear view.

Carrying our tea, we walked back to inspect the ground under the overhang. As the old man had predicted, there was one grapefruit-sized rock and several softball-sized rocks on the ground where our tent would have been. Happily, we had taken the old man's advice.

With no sun, there was no way to dry the tent, so we shook it out and packed it away wet. Fortunately, most of the rest of our gear had stayed dry. We struggled into our packs and headed up the trail. We were, in theory, losing elevation as we hiked down the gorge. But the trail led us up switchbacks and more switchbacks before heading down again, a feat of engineering in the precipitous terrain.

By early afternoon, the weather cleared and the sun came out. As we rounded a corner into the largest side-canyon entering this side of the gorge, a waterfall roared down multiple levels of limestone, worn into towers and smooth-sided pools. The opposite side of the gorge was covered by green plants, despite the steepness of the walls and lack of soil. In places, waterfall channels had been worn slick and reflected the sunlight like mirrors.

We came upon a sign on the edge of the only village in the gorge, Walnut Garden: "Welcome Stop, Guesthouse, Restaurant, Hostmen is Friendly Helpful and Speaks English." A stream flowing down from the mountain above and springs provide the water required for habitation. A woman washing clothes in a bucket in the dirt patio of the guesthouse cried out and a smiling man in his mid-twenties flew around the corner of the house to welcome us. Wang could not have been more delighted to see Westerners. His guesthouse, the only one in the gorge, has never been overbusy. Since the events at Tiananmen Square, he has had a hard time of it. Westerners give him valuable currency for lodging and dinners he cooks himself. Wang also has a mule for hire. Wang is learning English from one small grammar book, a pocket dictionary and his guests.

Although we had our tent with us and had carried enough food to eat, we decided to stay at Wang's guesthouse. It would have seemed churlish not to. We also hired Wang and his mule for the next day's trek.

By local standards, Wang is a prosperous man. He has a house and guesthouse made of stone, light from a lone electric bulb at night, a radio, a mule, a pig, a few chickens and some cornfields. He has a strong, hard-working wife, and three healthy daughters—five, three, and two years old. In the afternoon, the five-year-old struggled with a bucket of water she carried into the house from the spring just behind it. Later she carried in an armful of onions she had picked for our dinner. She is the oldest of three girls in a country where girl children are considered inferior because they cannot work as hard as men. She and her mother belie the supposition.

Inside his stone house, Wang cooked dinner for us on a fire built on the dirt floor. There was no chimney and smoke escaped through a hole in the roof. He chopped onions, fried them and scrambled eggs fresh from his hens. We sat on a blanket next to the fire and savored our meal. The rest of the family was conspicuously absent.

In the morning, by the time the gray clouds had lightened enough to see, Wang and his mule, Rick and I were on our way to the downstream mouth of the gorge. Despite the constant, low roar of the Yangtze in the bottom of the gorge, there is no water along the path. Although the configuration of the land is much more hospitable than in the steeper areas of the gorge that requires terraces to farm, this land is unusable. We walked through a desert, within earshot of one of the mightiest rivers in the world.

"The boatman on the ferry across the Yangtze is ruining my business," Wang complained. "He is so unreliable and charges rates so high, the tourists will not cross the river to hike up the gorge to stay at my guesthouse. But," he went on, "that is nothing compared to the disastrous effects of the what the central government did at Tainanmen Square. There have been so few tourists because of that. My family and I have suffered, even here." It was not a question of politics, human rights or freedom of expression for Wang. He was focussed on the direct financial impact Tiananmen Square had had on his family's well-being.

When we reached the mouth of the canyon, we paused for one last view. We looked past a walnut tree overhanging a garden, its wooden gate embedded in a stone wall. Prickly pears grew in the garden alongside banana trees. Beyond the garden, the cliffs of Tiger Leaping Gorge rose to the mountaintops, once again lost in clouds.

The trail through Tiger Leaping Gorge is a moderate trek. The path is narrow and steep, but it is a path. It is not extremely difficult, but it is not accessible to everyone. And that inaccessibility adds to its value. We knew we were fortunate to have had this opportunity.

The trail switch-backed down to the river. Road construction workers headed up the hill. We could see a couple of Westerners among the crowd on the other side of the river, but the ferryman would not allow them to get in his boat. Potential customers for Wang, so near, yet impossibly far away.

The ferryman delivered his load of passengers—Chinese only—to our side. We clambered aboard. The handsome young ferryman, a baby strapped to his back, headed the open forty-foot motor boat back up the eddy. I looked down into the swirling brown water. Skillfully, he headed the bow of the boat into the current, allowing the powerful river—its strength felt clearly here even miles below the gorge—to pull the boat downstream to the bottom of the eddy on the other side. The boat chugged up to the top of the eddy. Taking one last look at the Yangtze, watching the construction workers reach the top of the hill, I felt bereft. Few others will see Tiger Leaping Gorge as we did. I will not come this way again.

Orphans on Top of the World
~

A sense of spirituality pervades Dolpo. In the high Himalaya, thousand-foot cliffs tower over narrow trails winding down to rushing rivers far below. In these immense mountains, a person is insignificant. The presence of a greater power is clear. At every river crossing, on every ridge crest and mountain pass, travelers have constructed shrines—called *chortens*—in acknowledgement. Each one who passes by adds a rock to the base of the *chorten*, giving thanks for safe passage.

In July 2003, my two daughters, Laney, 22, and Piper, 18, and I trekked with Lama Tenzin, a Tibetan Buddhist monk, from Jomsom to Tsharka in Upper Dolpo. We were researching a book about the orphanage Lama Tenzin directs in Dehra Dun, India. The eleven children there had been identified by Dolpo village leaders as those facing the harshest circumstances. Several of the children's parents had died; some girls had been sold as workers. Others had suffered from severe malnutrition. Lama Tenzin and his family established a home for these children on a piece of family property in India. There, the children are raised in a Tibetan household and attend an excellent Indian private school.

The four of us flew from Dehli to Kathmandu, took a bus to Pokhara and flew to 9,000-foot-high Jomsom. From Jomsom, we walked in the shadow of cliffs up the deepest gorge in the world, Kali Gandaki. The footpath followed the banks of the roiling river. In places, it had swallowed the path, so we scrambled up the steep bank to a ledge, traversed the crumbling hillside, and dropped back down to the river. Others had been forced to make the same tenuous detour. As we passed, we added our own rocks to an elaborate *chorten* under an overhang in the cliff wall.

At four the next morning, the woman proprietor of the inn at Eklibatti tied *katas* (ceremonial scarves) around our necks and smeared butter in our hair, wishing us a safe journey. For three days, we hiked from early morning until dark, then dropped, exhausted, into our tent.

July is monsoon season in the Himalaya. It rains every day. The only difference is what time it starts. On the fourth day, we climbed the lower summit of Sangda La pass. At 16,000 feet, we moved very slowly, hesitating with each step to take another breath. Torrential rain kept us from crossing the second, higher summit.

The next morning, we climbed to 16,500 feet and descended the gentler western slope of the pass. We ate lunch at the yak herders' encampment at Molum Sumna. The herders spend four months there each summer, grazing their herds at high elevation.

The sixth day of our trek, we reached the village of Tsharka, a medieval town built entirely of stone. The flat roofs of the houses are trimmed in twisted shrubs, pulled up for firewood. In this region, high above timberline, there are no trees. Dried yak dung and tiny shrubs provide fuel. The first child we encountered was a small girl, staggering under the weight of a heavy metal water jug.

We pitched our tent at the Bon Po Monastery. During the days we spent in Tsharka, Lama Tenzin learned that the little girl we had first seen, six-year-old Choenyi, worked all day carrying burdens in return for food. Her unmarried mother, Karma, worked as a maid. She and Choenyi had no home of their own. After hours of conferences with village leaders, Lama Tenzin offered Choenyi the twelfth bed in the orphanage and Karma a job in the kitchen.

During these meetings, the village leaders made it clear that Tsharka wanted its own school. I agreed to help Tsharka meet this goal. In September I met Leona Mason, a teacher who has been working toward the same goal for several years, and we began working with the non-profit organization Room to Read, toward our goal of building an elementary school in Tsharka in the summer of 2004.

When we left Tsharka, Choenyi and Karma came with us. For the return trek, we each had a horse to ride. Where the trail was too steep, everyone walked. The morning we left Tsharka, as all of us were scrambling up a steep slope, one of the horses dislodged a large rock far above Piper and me. Time slowed as the boulder bounced closer and closer--then directly at me. I dove out of the way. I landed on my elbow, shattered it, hit my head and knocked myself out. When Piper got to me, she thought I was dead. I came to and opened my eyes. I thought I was blind. All I could see was bright white. As my pupils adjusted, Laney and Piper and Lama Tenzin came into focus.

The girls tied their scarves as slings around my right arm and immobilized it next to my body. Our horse packer, Tsultrim, with great kindness and skill, maneuvered me up to the top of the slope. He and Lama Tenzin pulled and pushed me into the saddle.

It started raining in early afternoon. By the time we reached Molum Sumna, we were drenched and shaking with cold. The yak herders welcomed us into their tent and served us sweet milk tea and grilled chapattis. We spend the night next to their tiny stove.

Three days later, we reached the Kali Gandaki gorge. We looked across the gorge to the snow-covered summit of Nilgiri. Before we descended to the river, we paused at a large *chorten*. With my good hand, I added a rock to its base, giving thanks for our safe return.

Note: *Children of Dolpo*, with fifty-five photos taken by Piper Crowell and text written by Euser, was published in December 2003 by the Writers Center of Marin. The school in Tsharka functioned in a tent during the late summer of 2003, directed by Leona Mason. The school building was completed in 2004 and has recently been rebuilt. In its seventeenth year of operation, sixty-five children attend the school, in classes ranging from kindergarten to grade seven.

~
CHAPTER TWO
~

Political Considerations

Reflections on Burning a Cocaine Lab

~

A machine-gunner of the Colombian National Police sits next to me in the doorway of the Bell 212 helicopter. The door is open—easier to return fire if necessary. Secured only by a seat belt, I scrunch back into the bench as far as I can.

For an hour we have been flying over an endless expanse of *silva*—layers of tree canopies varying from dark green to chartreuse. The dense forest is broken only by occasional patches of cleared ground with tin-roofed houses glinting in the sun. Two anti-narcotics policemen wielding machine guns, the pilot, co-pilot, and six U.S. government officials fill this helicopter. I am the only woman. I represent the Department of State. Others represent the Departments of Justice and Treasury. A second helicopter carrying a full complement of policemen flies ahead.

We are looking for coca fields. The police hope they will find a lab to burn. That would make this expense of blade time and exposure to danger even more worthwhile. But the primary purpose of this flight is to give our small group of Washington officials a direct experience in the Colombian fight against cocaine. Each of us plays a role in the decision-making process of how much anti-narcotics assistance Colombia will receive from the United States government—and which group, police or military—will receive it.

We fly over a field of coca being harvested. Eight men and women with half-full bags move slowly, deliberately through the field. They strip the branches of the coca bushes as though milking a cow. The leaves come off in their hands. They drop them in cloth bags suspended from one shoulder. It reminds me of pictures I have seen in history books of slaves harvesting fields of cotton. Once all the branches of one bush are stripped, the picker movers on to the next.

The police are not looking for a confrontation, although this is not a friendly visit. Our machine-gunner fires a few rounds into the forest. Five minutes from the first field, the pilot identifies another field, now uninhabited.

The first helicopter drops into this coca field, which has been completely harvested. As the first helicopter lands, our helicopter flies in circles, covering the police as they run out across the field, cradling their machine guns. The first helicopter rises and circles, covering us as our helicopter lands and we jump out. As soon as we are clear, it takes off. It can only protect us from above.

I am not thinking, just doing as I am told. If I allowed myself to think, I would be afraid. Or maybe I would ask myself if these policemen with machine guns are really necessary. Perhaps they are part of a show, a piece of performance theater in which the spectators also play a role. Is there really someone out there who would shoot us, if we weren't so well protected?

Immediately, the police stake out the edges of the field. We *norteamericanos* are left alone in the field wandering aimlessly, picking a few overlooked leaves, smelling them, tasting them. I suddenly feel very alone. Completely exposed. The helicopters continue circling above us.

One policeman goes to inform the inhabitants of the house on the edge of the field that, as long as they don't resist, the police will not do anything to harm them or the house. Three men and a woman stand dejectedly, leaning against the raised porch. One man is fat and shirtless. Another is thin and wears a green shirt and straw hat. A stout woman wears a skirt and a red sweater, its sleeves unraveling. The third fellow seems to shrink, hiding from our curious eyes.

Then the major yells and gestures *"Par alla!"* (Over there!) Relieved to have somewhere to go to escape the open field, we follow him like ducklings into the woods. I glance at the hollow base of a huge banana tree. Hidden in the shadows, a black policeman is poised on one knee, machine gun raised. The whites of his eyes seem to glow. He startles me.

The major leads us to a shed in the canopy of the trees. The tin roof is dark red, making it invisible from above. We scramble over a log across the small creek. The major politely offers me his hand, and helps me up the muddy slope below the cocaine lab.

The *"cocina"* (kitchen) is just a tin roof over a wooden floor on stilts. Chopped cocaine leaves lie drying over half the floor. A weed chopper with a large, improvised double blade has fallen half out of the shed. Five 55-gallon drums, full of chopped coca leaves mixed with gasoline, are lined up in one corner. A coca presser and a heap of coca residue cascade from the end of the shed closest to the barrels.

~ *Political Considerations* ~

The major pulls out a well-worn notebook. He carefully writes down a description of the lab, the number of barrels, an estimate of the quantity of drying leaves. We officials in our khaki pants, tennis shoes, and baseball caps are dressed as though we were going to a ball game. Instead, we listen attentively as the major describes the processing of cocaine. He scatters some cement from a bag on the floor over the chopped-up coca leaves to demonstrate how lime is used to dry the leaves and commence extraction of the alkaloid. After three days, the desiccated leaves are put into a drum and covered with gasoline.

I try to focus on the major's detailed description. His English is not perfect, but there are plenty of props at hand. He succeeds in making us understand the story. A broom handle with an open plastic waffle attached to it rests across the gasoline-filled barrels. The major explains that it is used to stir the coca mash. After three days of soaking, the gasoline has leached the cocaine alkaloid from the leaves. A wooden press is used to extract the last drop of cocaine-laden liquid from the leaves. I have seen similar wooden presses in other places. There they were used for the more benign purpose of forming adobe bricks.

The precious liquid is saved, the major continues, and the leaf residue is piled onto the growing heap of waste. Using chemicals, the alkaloid will be precipitated out of the liquid. The paste, or cocaine base, that is left will be moved to another location to be transformed into cocaine hydro-chloride—the white powder we call cocaine. Or the base may be sold as "*basuco*" and smoked.

The major estimates each fifty-five-gallon barrel will yield twenty-five to thirty kilos of base. The ratio of cocaine base to cocaine HCl is 1.1:1. Thus, each of the five barrels in this shed will yield twenty-three to twenty-seven kilos of cocaine powder. One hundred and fifteen to one hundred and thirty-five kilos of cocaine at $30,000 per kilo—street price in New York—equals $3,500,000 to $4,000,000. I am impressed. This little tin shed in the Colombian *silva* contains the makings of four million dollars worth of cocaine.

The major finishes his explanation and we Washington bureaucrats slip and slide down the short muddy slope, hop across the small stream, and walk back thoughtfully into the barren coca field. This operation is about to be destroyed.

The major and his men stay behind to torch the lab. First, a thread of smoke appears, then the drums of gasoline catch. A ball of flame glows through the trees. The heat of the fire rushes past us. Black chemical smoke blocks the sun, as we hurry to the helicopter that has just landed in the field.

Quickly, I clamber aboard behind the others. We rise and circle as the other helicopter lands and the camouflage-uniformed policemen run toward it. We keep circling until the second helicopter is safely in the air. As we head back over the *silva*, four figures walk slowly and sadly from the house across the stripped field to the charred remains of the lab.

The police have just destroyed their livelihood. But all is not lost. In six months, in the sun and the rain, the coca bushes will regrow their leaves. In six months, the people from the house and neighboring field will build a new lab.

Our two helicopters, like noisy voracious insects, fly across the vast *silva*. The multicolored canopies of trees give way to bright green fields of grass, dotted by cows and palm trees, stretching to the brown water of the Putumayo River. Far away from the river are small patches of fields. Now they all look like coca fields to me. Every tin roof is a lab. Hundreds of patches dotting the forest canopy of the *silva*. All in varying shades of green.

Helping with Bosnian Elections

~

At six o'clock in the morning, wispy gray clouds hung low below the tops of the hills. As the predawn sky lightened, Goran, my interpreter, Azul, my driver, and I approached the Bosian Serb town of Panjik. Azul slowed to a crawl to negotiate the potholes in the road between fields marked with the yellow tape of a de-mining operation. We passed through the former front lines between Bosnian and Serb-held territory. Azul pulled up in front of the Ambulanta, an outpatient clinic and community center newly built by the United States Agency for International Development (USAID).

On November 11, 2000, four days after the U.S. presidential election, I was in Lukavac municipality, near Tuzla, Bosnia, serving as a election supervisor under the auspices of the Organization for Security and Cooperation in Europe (OSCE). All the OSCE election supervisors had been in Bosnia for about a week. With my international colleagues and Bosnian interpreters, we had watched the U.S. election results on an overhead television set in our hotel lobby. We were engrossed with the ongoing situation in Florida, hanging chad, and election ambiguities. I had endured a lot of

~ *Political Considerations* ~

teasing, and some barbed remarks, about being an American presuming to monitor another country's election.

The 1995 Dayton Peace Accords had charged the OSCE with organizing and overseeing elections in Bosnia until elections could be carried out freely and fairly without international oversight. Working with municipal election committees, the OSCE had spent months preparing for these elections. November 11 was election day.

The polling committee was at work inside the unheated building—there was a space for a wood stove, but it had not yet been installed. Bright fluorescent lights welcomed us into the chilly room. The polling chairman—shirt, tie and sweater tucked neatly underneath his winter jacket—greeted us enthusiastically: "Dobro jutro!" ("Good morning!"). As we worked out way around the room, each committee member stopped rubbing his hands together for warmth in order to shake ours. The chairman then sent the junior committee member out for coffee.

The polling station was set up exactly according to instructions. A table with the voter registration book was just inside the door, followed by a table where ballots would be distributed. The cardboard voting screens, taped securely to the tops of square tables, were set up at the far end of the room, away from prying eyes. The election would be conducted entirely by hand. Pens were attached to each voting booth with string, lest they disappear. The ballot box was on another table in the center of the room, in clear view of all.

The committee member returned with a tray of little pots of thick Bosnian coffee (just like Turkish coffee, although it cannot be referred to as such in this part of the world), tiny cups and saucers, a Ballantine's bottle and shot glasses. We all gratefully accepted the tiny cups and added heaping teaspoons of sugar.

"You like?" the chairman proffered the Ballantine's bottle.

"No thanks," I regretfully declined. Only one committee member asked for a shot—at sixy-thirty a.m.—but I sympathized with him. Had I not been there in an official capacity, I would have joined him, just to feel the warmth of the alcohol in my throat. The liquid poured from the Scotch bottle was absolutely clear—local plum brandy, *slivovitz*—the bottle simply evidence of careful postwar recycling.

The polling committee took turns voting. Then, at seven o'clock, the polling station was officially open. In this small town, one hundred voters had registered. They were all Bosnian Serbs.

Before the war, a majority of the townspeople were Serb. When the war started, Serbs from what is now Republika Srpska pushed through this rural district, looting and burning all the Muslim homes. When the Bosnian army pushed back, the Serbs mined the front line and retreated. Then the advancing Bosnians looted and burned all the Serb homes. By the end of the war, only the floors and a few walls remained of the town's homes and surrounding farms.

After the war, international funds poured in to rebuild and repopulate the town. New houses had been built next to ruins. Serbs who had lived in camps for displaced persons since they were driven out are slowly returning, family by family. A doctor came to the Ambulanta two days a week. There was electricity. Telephones worked Monday through

~ *Political Considerations* ~

Friday during business hours. A school was under construction. A few plum trees still grew. And, for the first time since the Dayton Peace Accords were signed in December 1995, Panjik had its own polling station.

This was my fourth trip to Bosnia as an elections supervisor, a volunteer position I'd applied for through the U.S. Department of State, which provides the U.S. delegation of supervisors to the OSCE. Since my first experience in 1997, Bosnians' ability to manage elections had improved dramatically. The September 1997 election, the first in which I worked, was the second since the war had ended. Other volunteers who had worked the 1996 election were full of horror stories about the level of disorganization. The second time around, many logistical problems had been solved, such as how to distribute blank ballots to the polling stations and how to transport and store marked ballots. But the local election committees were still just learning how to run a polling station, how to deal with questions about whether a voter was registered or not and how to count the ballots efficiently at the end of the polling period. International supervisors were actively engaged in the election—we answered questions and made suggestions to the polling station's committee chairman and participated in the process. By the November 1997 election, the local election committees were better at their jobs—there were fewer questions, less confusion—and by 1998, polling station management was practically routine.

In 2000, international supervisors were each given four polling stations to oversee instead of just one. Under the new arrangement, we would spent only twenty-five percent of our time at each site. The OSCE had calculated correctly. Constant oversight by an elections supervisor at each polling station was no longer required.

Voters trickled into the polling station. In this small town, each voter was well known by each committee member, and the voters invariably shook hands with the committee members and with Goran, Azul and me before taking their ballots behind the cardboard voting screen. Azul radioed to the municipal district headquarters that Panjik polling station had opened on time and was operating smoothly.

The mist below the hilltops had evaporated with the arrival of the sun. On the hillsides, trees blazed red in the morning light. Five years ago, the red blazes in these hills were burning homes.

We left the polling station in the quiet sunrise. Peace reigned in Panjik.

The warm car felt cozy after the chilly polling station. Azul headed down the dirt road toward the much larger town of Turija, our second polling station. Again, he carefully negotiated the potholes, past the yellow de-mining cape, into the town. Turija was never taken by the Serbs. There is not much damage evident in the homes, shops or school. The polling station occupied one of the classrooms in the town's grade school.

About thirty voters were waiting in line when we arrived. The committee member who was supposed to be in charge of crowd control was not doing a very effective job—some folks were elbowing their way to the front of the line, angering those who had waited patiently. It seemed to me, however, that there was not much to be mad about.

~ *Political Considerations* ~

The voters were waiting in the hall inside the school, and outside it was sunny and beginning to get warm. In 1997 and 1998, voters had stood in a line for hours in the rain in order to vote. But as voting has become more routine, the voters have become more demanding. And maybe that is right.

I observed a similar phenomenon within the polling committee at Turija. Committees were composed of members of both major parties, and some smaller parties. The older members of the Turija committee were from the SDA, the traditional nationalist Muslim party. The younger, more energetic members were from the SDP, the multi-ethnic party generally favored by the international community. In previous elections, committee members were so pleased to be part of the election process, there was no squabbling among them. However, splits and schisms were becoming evident as elections became routine. I was assigned to attend the vote count that night at Turija—the municipal election headquarters had done a good job of identifying which of my polling stations was most likely to have problems.

Everyone in line was anxious to vote. Voters of all ages participated. Based on their clothes, the twenty-somethings could have been in England or Germany. Most middle-aged voters were in well-worn coats and slacks or dresses. Old women from the countryside wore the long skirts of flowing material gathered in at the hem that look like harem pants.

It was only later that I reflected on who was missing at the polling stations. Where were the young men who were injured in the war—*mutilés de la guerre*? When I had supervised other elections, they were voting. If a veteran was in a wheelchair, it was carried up the stairs by his friends. In one voting station, the ballot box had been moved to the floor so that handicapped voters could drop their ballot into the box without having to ask for assistance. This time, injured veterans were conspicuously absent. Like other evidence of the war, they seem to have disappeared.

Our next polling station was at Bikodze. There was no commercial center in this town, only a couple of small shops. Each stucco house was surrounded by a garden plot and grass, mowed by a few sheep or a couple of cows. An outdoor table was located either under a grape arbor or a fruit tree, next to a double-decker wooden chicken coop. The hills rolled gently through the countryside, and on a sunny November day, it was easy to see why people would fight to control this fertile land.

The polling station was located in the cultural center. The glass-fronted building housed a large meeting room and a stage. The large room was nearly filled with long sections of gray plastic pipe for the town's new water system. The polling tables and voting booths were squashed into a narrow section of the room. The overhead lights were not working, so even mid-morning, the room was in semi-darkness. And it was almost as cold inside as it had been at six o'clock that morning in the polling station at Panjik.

Each table and voting booth had its own lamp so voters could see to mark their ballots. When older voters had trouble reading the ballots, they would ask another voter, or a member of the committee, to borrow their glasses. Glasses were traded from booth to booth, then back to their owner. *Nema problema*—no problem.

The wide cement porch was heated by the sun, and people lingered there to chat. One of the polling committee members, a garrulous fellow with a wide gaping smile, complained to me that party representatives were loitering on the porch, accosting voters and intimidating them on their way inside. According to the election rules, no party solicitation or signs are allowed within fifty yards of the polling station. As the international observer assigned to this station, I had the authority to take action against the party solicitors. Through Goran, I informed them of the fifty-yard rule. Since there was no marker, I determined that the fence surrounding the polling station was about the right distance. Grumbling good-naturedly, they slouched into position outside the fence.

Our fourth station, Prokosovici, on the shore of Lake Modrac, was located on the second floor of a former nightclub—or at least that was how the large murals of semi-clothed women on all four walls were explained to me. Despite the décor, this polling station was extremely well organized and efficient. Six cardboard polling screens taped to tables were lined up along one wall. There were three ballot boxes, each with a ballot corresponding to a separate race taped to its top. There was nothing in the rules about separate boxes, but this setup would save a lot of time separating ballots that night. The woman who was directing voters to unoccupied booths also made sure voters deposited each ballot in the appropriate box before exiting.

The stocky, affable chairman was solidly engaged in overseeing the operation. The queue, which formed outside the room and trailed down the stairs, was kept gently but firmly in check by the committee member at the door.

The woman who handed out the ballots impressed me. Using the same polite phrases with each voter, she described which race each of the three ballots was for and instructed voters to mark only one party, or candidates from only one party, on each ballot. I watched her repeat this performance during each of my visits to the polling station that day. There were nine hundred and twenty-two registered voters in this precinct. She repeated herself nine hundred and twenty-two times, never varying her polite, clear instructions. I was sorry we could not stay at Prokosovici for the count—it would be quick and efficient.

Outside the window of the polling station, the lake surface glinted in the winter sun. A family passed along the cement promenade, the boy gliding by on in-line skates. Not much evidence of the war here.

Voting was an excuse for a family outing. Parents brought their children to the polls. At Prokosovici, a mother's heavy stockinged legs were visible under one screen. Under the screen next to her were the skinny legs of a little girl in knee socks who was studiously observing her mom. At Turija, a little boy, tucked under his father's arm, dropped his father's ballot in the box. The next generation of voters was in training.

We made the rounds of the four polling stations again. In Panjik, I asked the chairman which party would win his town. "For us, there is no contest," he replied. "There is only one party to vote for—SDP. We are Serbs. We will not vote for the SDA."

In Bikozde, the local party hacks had removed themselves from directly outside the fence and were drinking outside a house on a rise overlooking the cultural center.

They shouted at me when I arrived, asking if they were far enough away. Goran didn't need to explain. It was a taunt, but I waved at them in what I hoped they would understand was a friendly fashion and shouted, "*Dobro!*" ("Good!").

Just before the polls closed, we returned to Turija. The chairman locked the door and the committee began the count. With three separate ballots, the count was complicated. First, the committee separated the ballots into three stacks. Then each stack was separated according to the party marked. Each party's votes were double-counted and the results entered on a master tally sheet. Counted ballots were secured with rubber bands and placed in nylon bags for transport to the municipal district headquarters. Slowly, laboriously, the committee worked into the night. The grumbling between party members escalated. I mediated. Goran and I helped the chairman sort ballots, working around the edges of the table.

As the count progressed, it was clear that in this precinct the multi-ethnic SDP was not doing as well as the international community hoped it would. In municipal elections in April 2000, the SDP had shown strong gains against the nationalist SDA. The international community was dreaming of the SDP continuing its rise to prominence. However, the SDA, which had controlled the country throughout the war, was making a strong showing.

At three o'clock in the morning, the count was completed. The SDP had won, but by only a narrow margin. Committee members telephoned in the results to their respective parties. We were all too tired to celebrate. The chairman and his deputy loaded the bags of ballots into their car to take them to headquarters. As we shook hands one final time, the representative of the SDP smilingly asked, "Now that you have helped us with our elections, maybe we should come help you with yours?"

Running the Zagreb Marathon
~

"You're going to run a marathon where?" my husband was incredulous.

"Zagreb," I repeated, less confidently than the first time I had announced my intention.

"Why not Venice?" he challenged, reaching the crux of the matter.

Not Venice, because running the Zagreb marathon was not just a marathon in a lovely city. I have run marathons in Paris, Washington, D.C. and Denver, Colorado, and enjoyed them all. I have been part of the crowd of runners, participating in the event, rejoicing in the energy and esprit inevitably shared. I wanted to run the Zagreb marathon because I have Croatian friends, because I have felt helpless during the duration of the war, and in this small way, I wished to express my support for the end of madness and a return to normal life.

Sporting events are one symbol of normal life and acceptance in the events is evidence of a country's acceptance by the community—or rejection. Thus, South Africa was excluded from participating in international sports events while it persisted in its policy of apartheid. The Federal Republic of Yugoslavia (Serbia Montenegro) was prohibited from participating as long as it maintained its belligerent position towards Croatia and Bosnia-Hertzegovina. When Belgrade finally indicated its willingness to stop supporting the Bosnian Serbs in the Balkan war, the United Nations agreed to lift sanctions by degrees. The first sanction to be lifted permitted athletes of the Federal Republic of Yugoslavia to participate in international sports events. I wondered if any Serbs would run in the Zagreb marathon—if personal will exists among Serbian runners for reconciliation with their Croatian fellow-athletes.

    I am a recreational runner. Over the twenty-six-point-two mile marathon course (forty-two-point-two kilometers), I am delighted to average ten-minute plus miles. I participate for the pleasure of the experience, and to remember what I was doing during that particular four-and-one-half hours of my life. The Zagreb marathon brochure clearly stated "Course duration: four hours." I already knew I couldn't finish in four hours. I remembered my first marathon in Denver. The race barriers were taken down after five hours. At five hours and twenty minutes, I limped over the finish line. I imagined a similar thing might happen in Zagreb. Humiliating, but unavoidable: I run slowly. But I was not deterred.

    When I picked up my race packet, I realized the Zagreb marathon would be different than any I had run before. There were not thousands of participants milling around. The race list comprised only a hundred or so competitors, with very few women. There appeared to be five Americans. A number of runners had listed UNCRO—the United Nations forces in Croatia—as their address. These runners from UNCRO were charged with keeping peace between

~ Political Considerations ~

Croatians and Serbs who had over-run Croatian territory in 1991, until the Croatians forced the Serbs out in the summer of 1995. They will not be here for next year's marathon.

Like much of life in a country at war, running in Zagreb is serious. Recreational running is undeveloped, although the local running clubs had tried to remedy that by including two-kilometer and five-kilometer "fun runs" at the start of the marathon. My Croatian friends living near me in Paris had been surprised to learn of the fourth annual Zagreb marathon. However, in a four-inch news item, yesterday's Saturday edition of the Zagreb morning paper "Vjesnik," had declared runners from Norway, Slovenia, Moldova, Hungary, and Britain would be running in the marathon, and listed four world-ranked runners who would vie to win.

Taking the train from the Central Square Sunday morning to the marathon start, I met Zoran, the only other rider dressed in running gear. At the starting line, he introduced me to Daniel and half a dozen other members of his running club, including one woman runner. Everyone was stretching, adjusting clothing, pinning on race numbers. I identified the other Americans, who told me they were working temporarily at a hospital near Zagreb—their presence, like the UNCRO runners, attributable to the war.

The morning was cool and overcast. The volume of enthusiasm generated by thousands of runners, as in Paris, was replaced by a collegial club spirit. About one hundred marathoners, two wheel-chair racers, several hundred school children, and five-kilometer runners massed behind the start line. With the starting shot, enthusiastic kids running two kilometers sped past marathoners pacing themselves for the long haul. At five kilometers, most of the field peeled off and returned to the stadium finish-line. The rest of us pressed forward, running next to the Zagreb tramline. I paced myself behind two other Americans, a man and a woman, at the end of the pack. At ten kilometers, the woman dropped out, and the man shot forward to catch up with the rest of the runners. Though I feared I was the last of the runners, I knew better than to try and catch him. I could finish this marathon in good condition if I kept to ten-minute miles. At the first water stop, I realized I was only next-to-last: a woman was chatting loudly with the final motorcycle escort as she climbed the hill. I was greatly relieved—briefly.

Running down the hill, voices got louder behind me. I felt it would be unbearable to run at the absolute end of the marathon alone with a motorcycle escort, the emergency medical van on my heels, stopping traffic all the way. I had to keep up with this small powerhouse of a woman. I picked up my pace slightly as she drew alongside, and felt a surge of energy as we ran together. I had heard her bantering in Croatian. We established that as an American, I spoke English and French, as a German she spoke German and Croatian: we had no common language. She held up six fingers and said "ein kilometer." I was delighted and relieved: six minutes per kilometer equals ten minutes per mile. "Okay! Good!" Now, instead of feeling embarrassed to be at the end of the race, with Brigitta I became part of a unique duo of over-45-year-old foreign women in this serious marathon. Brigitta maintained an extremely disciplined pace. Using sign language and reciting place names, Brigitta informed me she had run marathons in a string of European cities, as well as in New York.

~ *Political Considerations* ~

Initially, the route ran through city streets, past St. Stephen's, Zagreb's largest cathedral, skirting the Central Square and out into the suburbs. Evidence of the shelling of Zagreb had been quickly repaired. We saw no signs of the destruction I knew remained only a few kilometers distant. At mid-point we ran around a lake in a large park next to the Sava River. Crews were sculling on the tranquil lake; joggers and walkers followed the path on top of the river embankment. The recent Balkan war was far away.

At twenty miles, Brigitta and I started passing other runners. Our slow but steady pace was paying off. The mopping-up motorcycle escort and emergency van dropped back. We followed the well-marked route through small streets along the edge of town, houses on one side and market-gardens on the other. Home gardeners favored pink and red roses and fluffy lemon-yellow dahlias as large as dinner plates. Girls and boys lined up alongside the street to give Brigitta and me high-five's as we passed. Older men looked at us as though we were crazy. Women clapped and called out "Bravo!"

At the finish line, at four hours and nineteen minutes—my personal best—the only people left were the woman logging in times and the man who hung finishing medals around our necks. Brigitta and I hugged each other in celebration, then she left with her husband. We had not exchanged contact information. We felt no need. We had connected during one memorable marathon, then our paths parted. Zoran and Daniel approached with congratulatory hugs. I was touched that they had waited for me. We sat outside the cafe by the tennis courts and drank cappucinos and apricot juice.

We did not seem to be in a war zone, yet we inevitably, indirectly talked about it. Zoran, in his early twenties, had safely completed his obligatory military service and was studying to be a teacher. He would prefer to be training to do something else, but had found no better opportunities. He dreamed of joining his brother in Canada. Zoran was finished with the war and longed to move on. Daniel, by contrast, was in his late twenties and full of enthusiasm for his work: organizing sports activities, theatre productions, and art projects for teenagers at a refugee camp in Zagreb. Daniel's life revolved around the aftermath of war and equipping young refugees to return home and eventually build a tolerant, multi-ethnic society.

I came to Croatia to see as much as I could of this country which, with the other states of former Yugoslavia, has dominated world news for the past three years. I learned that, despite the effects of war, the country functions, running clubs sponsor marathons, young people study and pursue their careers. I came to Croatia to make my small contribution to the return to normalcy in Zagreb—which despite the unresolved madness of war—is well underway.

~

CHAPTER THREE

~

On Board

Across the Sea:
Letter Home from a Twenty-Nine-Day Transatlantic Sail

~

On November 2, 1999, I flew to London to prepare for a transatlantic crossing in my thirty-four-foot sailboat, Islander. At Heathrow, I met my crew, two young women, for the first time. Erika was a friend of a friend, Karson a friend of Erika's. Mid-Atlantic, I wrote a letter to my husband, Dean, my eighteen-year-old daughter Helane, and my fourteen-year-old daughter Piper...

> *One fine day a small ship sailed away*
> *Three sirens its captain and crew*
> *She was bound for the isles*
> *Of Caribbean style*
> *So across the Atlantic she flew*

~ On Board ~

December 3, 1999

Dean and Piper and Helane,

 Last night just after sunset, I was sitting in the cockpit with Karson. She mentioned some trinkets she had bought in Madeira for friends and family, and I realized I hadn't bought any trinkets for anyone. I don't like trinkets very much, but they do let people know you were thinking of them while traveling. I am thinking of you all the time. I've decided to give you a present of words in the form of a letter. It won't be chronological, because I am starting on day eighteen of the voyage. And it won't include everything, because that is not possible. But I will try to paint some word pictures for you so you can form an impression of the time I spent away from you.
 This is a good time to begin this letter, because we are sailing nearly downwind and the boat doesn't rock very much. It certainly doesn't plunge and buck the way it does when we are sailing into the wind. Today we are flying the "gennaker," a triangular spinnaker. We use it only in very light winds. It is made of lightweight nylon, and because of the way it is cut, it has stripes at the bottom, while at the top, the stripes become vees. It is a beautiful red and white balloon billowing out over the starboard life rails. The boat moves forward like a bird.
 Today, when we first raised the gennaker, the wind was puffing lightly from a different direction every few minutes. Erika had to hand steer for her whole three-hour watch because the winds kept shifting from east to southeast. I hand-steered my watch also. During Karson's watch, we were

able to set Henri, the Monitor self-steering mechanism. Gene Valentine and I named it Henri when we sailed from Chesapeake Bay to France. Since we are now on our way back to America, we usually call it Hank.

December 4, 1999

The only danger of flying a gennaker is having the wind rise and not pulling the sail in quickly enough. The sail can be ruined, or worse, someone could be injured in the struggle against the wind. We had to decide whether to leave the gennaker up during the night. The wind was light all day—under ten knots—and we were happy to be proceeding toward Antigua. We decided to leave it up, with the understanding that if the wind ever topped eleven knots during anyone's watch, that person would call the others so we could haul the gennaker down. The wind did not increase during the night, except for occasional gusts. Today the gennaker is still flying, and Hank is still at the helm.

Even when Hank is steering, we keep a twenty-four-hour watch. Each person takes three hours on, six hours off. That way, someone is always in the cockpit, keeping an eye on Hank, the sail, the boat in general, and a lookout for any ships that might be passing. We haven't seen a ship or even a sailboat for several days now. But earlier in the trip we would occasionally see one in the distance, and at times one has passed close by. Our first night out of Vilamoura, Portugal, we crossed the major shipping lane used by ships entering and departing the Mediterranean through the Straits of Gibralter. We did not see any of those ships close up, but once I counted the lights of eight ships along the lane.

~ *On Board* ~

From time to time, I feel anxious about arriving home. I send an e-mail message to you every day. I know they leave my machine, but I have no way of knowing whether they get to you. I must assume they do. I tried to contact you by radiotelephone a week ago on Sunday, but could never get the WLO folks to acknowledge me. I could hear them talking to other people. It was a very frustrating experience. I just wanted to tell you that we are fine, progressing across the Atlantic inch by inch.

On our chart of the Atlantic Ocean, the scale is such that one inch equals about sixty miles. On our best twenty-four-hour days, we have progressed two inches. On our worst days, less than one inch. Inch by inch, I am coming home to you.

This morning my watch was from nine a.m. to noon, Greenwich Mean Time. As we travel west, we are passing through time zones, so actually the watch was about seven a.m. to ten a.m. local time. That is, I saw the sunrise on the watch—a golden one with piles of gray clouds turned into treasure by the rising light. When the sun comes up, the wind becomes uncertain, changing directions back and forth. I hand steered for a while; then Hank was able to take over again.

I decided to make hot chocolate for myself in the cockpit while on watch. A simple thing on land, at sea, making a cup of hot chocolate requires mindful concentration. I went below and assembled what I needed: the Bluet camp stove; white enamel coffee pot; jar of matches; packet of Milkman powdered milk; box of Poulain hot chocolate mix from France. Using the brass handpump in the galley, I filled the coffee pot two-thirds full of water, then carefully carried it into the cockpit. I gripped the coffee pot between my feet so it wouldn't slide away or tip over while I lit the stove, but the precaution was probably unnecessary. We were once again sailing downwind in a light breeze, thus the boat was stable. I held the coffeepot on the stove, applying enough pressure to keep the stove from sliding around. As the water heated up, with my free hand I shook Milkman from the packet and spooned chocolate from its box into the coffeepot and stirred it around. When the hot chocolate was steaming, I turned off the stove and poured a cup's worth into the mug I'd bought in Rodetown, during our family vacation to the British Virgin Islands. I have such fond memories of that vacation; the mug holds a special significance for me.

Karson and Erika were asleep below. The only sounds were the whispering gurgle of Hank's rudder slicing through the water and occasional humph of wind spilling from the gennaker in a gust. It is incredibly peaceful and calm on a morning like this one, sitting in the cockpit sipping hot chocolate from a favorite mug, in our lovely boat, bound for the Caribbean.

Last evening's sunset was deep yellow-orange, reflecting off of dark gray clouds. At the horizon, a dark cloud was edged with golden light just as the sun dropped below the horizon. Each evening, we watch the sunset and hope to see the green flash people talk about. None of us has seen it yet on this trip. Karson saw it once in Hawaii, and Earl Seagers, the author of our weather book, confirms it exists and explains its causes. After the sun was gone, the gold-orange clouds changed to deep rose. They reflected rose light on the waves leading from the clouds to our boat. It reminded me of the alpine glow we saw on Mount Blanc in Chamonix.

~ On Board ~

During my three a.m. to six a.m. watch, the moon had not yet risen. Clouds obscured some of the stars, but many stars shone brightly. One especially bright star, having just risen, created a path of reflected light across the waves. The moon often creates such a light path—sometimes with a full moon it is more like a light lake. It is not so common with stars.

Today was another beautiful tropical sail. We took down the gennaker at dark last night because we could see an ominous dark cloud approaching. We raised the reefed main and pulled out the jib. Within minutes of our sail change, eighteen knot winds buffeted the boat. We sailed under jib and reefed main until this morning, when we raised the gennaker again. Winds were a little stronger today—eight to thirteen knots, still out of the southeast.

In a book I am reading called *We the Navigators*, about how stars, sun, wind and currents are used by South Sea Islanders instead of compasses for navigation, winds from different directions have different names. I thought about that last night, as the east and northeast winds were making an effort to gain dominance over the southeast wind. The islanders name the winds based on where they come from—thus last night it was Azorian Wind and Moroccan Wind that were fighting against Conakry Wind. The main filled and backfilled, but eventually Conakry Wind won the competition and strengthened, pushing us on our way.

Sleek dolphins arrive,
Speeding under rose-streaked skies,
Celebrating dawn.

December 6, 1999

This morning I stood the dark three a.m. to six a.m. watch. I was very sleepy as my watch ended, thinking only of going below for a nap. Then a dorsal fin cut through the water on the port side of the boat. Dolphins had come to pay us a visit. There were dozens of them. The sky was streaked with rose-colored clouds, and the dolphins joined us to celebrate the new day. They stayed with us for forty-five minutes. When Karson came to take over my watch, I went to the bow and lay down on my stomach so I could watch the dolphins racing along under the surface of the water. Suddenly, there was nothing better in the world to do than watch the dolphins and the sunrise.

The three of us later had coffee and tea in the cockpit. Then we tacked a difficult task.

Yesterday, when we took the gennaker down, the wind had started to gust. We had waited too long to drop the sail. Erika held onto the sheet as we rounded up into the wind and the force of the wind on the taut sail nearly tore it in two. Karson has unwrapped the gennaker halyard from the winch prematurely and was holding it in her hand when the force on the taut sail jerked the line through her hand, burning her. The sail dropped into the water, and we quickly pulled it into the boat before we ran over it. But the end of the halyard was up in the rigging. We stuffed the sail in its bag, then pulled the halyard down. The difficult task facing us this morning was to go up the mast and run the halyard through its block so that we could raise the gennaker again. I strapped on my climbing harness. Erika took the helm. In case the main halyard broke, I tied a safety prussig loop around the jib halyard. Then I clipped my harness into the main halyard.

Slowly and steadily, Karson winched me upwards. I gripped the mast with my legs and hugged it with my arms, but it was difficult to keep from swinging side to side as the boat rolled in the waves. We had chosen a calm moment for me to begin my ascent, but as Karson hauled me up, gusts of wind caused the boat to roll even more. When I finally reached the spreaders, I was shocked to see how much further I had to go. But Karson kept raising me, and I kept pushing the prussig loop up, with the spinnaker halyard coiled over my right arm. Finally, I reached the top of the mast, I then had to uncoil the halyard and feed it through the block. Of course, it tangled.

It took all my concentration to focus on what I had to do. Do not look at the water. Do not look at the horizon. Do not look at the little deck so far below. I untangled the halyard slowly, deliberately, feeding it through the block as the boat pitched and rolled. My legs were wrapped tightly around the mast. As soon as I dropped the end down to Karson, she cleated it off. Then I had to untangle the rest of the halyard. When the remainder of the line was finally free, it swung back and forth wildly. She tried to grab it each time it passed, but kept missing it. I wanted to go down, but Karson had to secure the halyard before she could lower me. Once, twice, three, four times it crossed the deck, then the halyard wrapped itself around a shroud. I tried to shake it loose. Finally, it came unwound and Karson grabbed it. She tied it off. Then she began lowering me cautiously toward the deck. Coming down, I got caught in the lazy jacks. Karson released the lazy jacks to free me. Gratefully, I stood on the deck again. We had made several mistakes we would not repeat.

> *Skim light over swells,*
> *Burrow deep in the next wave,*
> *Flying fish at play.*

December 7, 1999

Less than nine hundred miles to go. These will be difficult days. We left Funchal three weeks ago. We are three-quarters of the way through the voyage. But it's not over yet. We could still have storms, any number of problems. We're still a long way from port. We need to keep ourselves on this trip. We could easily start focusing on what we plan to do when we get to shore and lose the privilege of the last week at sea. Days could become days to endure, not savor. We are tired of being in this confined space. We are tired of not exercising. Our attempts to stretch in the cockpit or down below are a feeble substitute for walking or running. This part of the voyage has its own psychological challenges.

It was cloudy all day, offering us some relief from the tropical sun. On the weather net, we heard we may be in for a gale of thirty-plus knot winds, probably with rain. We may miss it, or we may find ourselves in the middle of it. We are preparing ourselves. Flew only the jib all day. Running downwind, we might be able to raise the main and sail wing-on-wing, but that would be tricky—demanding hand-steering—and it might not add that much speed. We are averaging four nautical miles made good per hour, and Hank is steering. We are tired, unwilling to hassle ourselves unnecessarily. Probably a sign of the last quarter of the voyage.

December 8, 1999

Before this voyage is over, I must tell you about the electrical squall. On the evening of day fifteen, we saw lightning flashes to the northwest and lightning flashes to the southeast. As the sun set, clouds built into black mountains. We expected rain and lightning. We discussed what measures we would take. The main thing was to keep ourselves from harm. The best way to do that was to stay in the cabin of the boat, out of the cockpit and away from all metal surfaces. Since Islander's wheel is metal, it would not be advisable to be hand-steering the boat with lightning flashing all around. Hank was set and had been steering for hours. Of course, in heavy weather, the wind is likely to change direction, and since Hank steers in relation to the direction of the wind, the boat would change direction, too. However, sailing for a few hours in the wrong direction was less of a problem than potential injury from being overly brave. We agreed that whoever was on watch when the lightning got close would come below.

Karson had the nine p.m. to midnight watch. She went out in full foul-weather gear, prepared for whatever might arrive. Erika and I tried to get some sleep, knowing that there could be an emergency if lightning hit the boat. I wasn't able to sleep, but lay dutifully stretched out on my berth, trying to let my body rest. About ten-thirty p.m., I saw flashes of light through the portals. The seas had risen and the boat was bucking through the waves. It was useless to pretend to rest. I got up to tell Karson to come below. We had put all the hatch boards in place to keep rain from getting into the cabin. To keep the cabin as dry as possible, I slid back the hatch cover just enough to peer over the top board.

My heart stopped. Karson was not in the cockpit. I stared at the empty space. The seas were high, but not crashing overboard. Where was she? Dear God! Had she been swept overboard? Then Karson whispered, giggling, "Here I am." In a flash of lightning, I saw her sitting curled up in the port berth. My heart began beating once again. I'd thought I couldn't sleep, but I must have been asleep when she'd come inside.

We watched the lightning strobe reflect off white-topped waves, illuminating the cockpit. None of us had ever seen such a display of electricity. No time elapsed between lightning flashes and thunderous roars.

We were dry and relatively safe inside the cabin, but my mind raced through worst-case scenarios. We could be hit by lightning. If the boat caught fire, we would try to extinguish it. If we failed, we would abandon the boat. That would mean getting my crew and myself into our life raft in the high wind and waves. Or we could be hit by lightning and suffer the loss of all of our electronics. No lights, no communications, no engine—we could figure out how to deal with that. Those would be small problems, compared to potential total disaster.

After four hours, the lightning flashes came minutes apart, rather than every few seconds. Heavy wind and rain continued, but it was time to check on Hank. Fully suited up, I crawled through the hatch boards and clipped the tether of my harness onto the jack line. Using my flashlight, I checked our jib, furled it into a small triangle of a sail. Hank was performing like a champion, keeping us on course relative to the wind. However, the wind had changed direction and was now blowing from the northwest. We were headed due south, not west to the Caribbean. Erika joined me in the cockpit and we redirected Hank. It was now technically my watch. I stayed in the cockpit in darkness and rain, contemplating the heavy weather.

> *Sunset's fuschia clouds*
> *Glow, reflect rose-hued on waves:*
> *Tropic seas, day's end.*

December 9, 1999

Today is a lovely, mild day. Sky mostly cloud-covered, balmy temperature, light wind. Unfortunately, the wind is out of the west—exactly the direction we need to go. We can't sail directly into the wind, so we head southwest. We are being pushed away from our destination of Antigua. We could tack back and forth across the wind, be we are all anxious to get home. We sail as close to the wind as we can, heading south of our target.

Last night there was a golden sunset, and dolphins came to join us once again. Karson and I sat at the bow of the boat, thinking how wonderful it is when the best use of our time is to fully savor a sunset and dolphins.

Overnight I had the midnight to three a.m. watch. Moonlit and quiet. Quite a few stars. Sailed under jib alone.

We had taken the main down at sunset, wanting to avoid wrestling with it during the night.

This morning, I had the nine a.m. to noon watch. We have sailed far enough west that the sun rises at ten a.m. GMT. I didn't start making my hot chocolate until the sunrise was complete. Sitting in the cockpit, I drank the chocolate slowly. Maybe that is the lesson I am learning out here: to savor each individual moment or event or project or meal. My life proceeds at a more stately pace. On land, I drink my coffee while I read the paper. I drive to the grocery store while listening to a French lesson on tape. Here there is no need to try to do more than one thing at a time. Hot chocolate can wait until I have watched the theatrical breaking of the new day.

> *Single star so bright*
> *Its path shines across the waves*
> *Seen only at sea.*

December 10, 1999

During the night, the glass bowl on the primary fuel filter broke. We tried various means to fix it: replacing it with a plastic cup; epoxying it back together; sealing the epoxied cup to the filter. It didn't work. Air gets into the fuel system. We spent a couple of hours trying to bleed it, unsuccessfully. So now we have no engine, no way to recharge the batteries. I am very discouraged. Was there some way to prevent the glass from breaking that I should have known about? Maybe it broke because it was full of water. Maybe I should have been draining it. Maybe it was just old. It seems there is al-

~ On Board ~

ways something more I need to know about sailing. Now we are engineless. We won't be able to use the single side band radio, send emails, or listen to tapes at night while we cook dinner. We'll have to cook before it gets dark. We must save the battery so that we can use our lights when we see a ship at night, so that we can use the VHF radio when we get to port or in case of emergency. Of course, many sailors sail without engines, using alternate means to charge their batteries. But our one panel of photovoltaic cells is not powerful enough to make much of a difference.

Bowing to the wind and weather, we have adjusted our objective and are headed to Barbados, four hundred miles away. But we need more wind. It is frustrating. We are anxious to get to our destination, but the wind blows from the wrong direction, or we have none. We are all studying patience. Maybe we will learn the lesson.

December 11, 1999

The concerns on a passage are basic. Is there enough wind from the right direction? Is there enough palatable water? What's for lunch, snacks, dinner? I like this about sailing. Problems are confined to the very small universe of the boat and items on it. We live at a slow pace, although I find there is always something to clean or fix or attend to between watches. With three people on board, there is also time to think and write. On watch especially, there is time to think and dream.

At home, I have a daily schedule, rituals. Here I have my rituals, too: taking our position at noon, plotting it on the chart, making a daily entry in the log book and the engine log, averaging our daily mileage. I write in my journal, compose an e-mail to you and send it forth on invisible wave lengths to a satellite I cannot see, hoping and believing you will receive it soon.

December 12, 1999

This may be my last sunrise watch on this passage. The sky brightened into golden fire. A parade of black clouds shaped like animals—a bear, a seal, an elephant—marched in front of the flames. The clouds in the west turned pink, flushed with expectation at the prospect of meeting the sun.

Passages are exceptional circumstances of sailing. Day sailing between anchorages or ports, we escape to the water for some hours, at night anchoring ourselves once again to the land. A passage is a physical separation from the earth for a prolonged period of time. We are surrounded by acres of water, fields of water; on days like today, hills and valleys of water. Unlike eternal mountains, the topography of the sea constantly changes. We have floated, untethered, for nearly thirty days. We are earthlings no more.

> *Thirty days sailing over the sea*
> *Through lightning, thunder, clouds and sun,*
> *Three sirens arrived*
> *Without feeling deprived*
> *In Barbados and laughed, sipping rum.*

Sailing the Singlehanded TransPac
~

"Turn right at the A in GALE." Sailors repeated the dark joke up and down the Corinthian Yacht Club docks. Most of us—the twenty-four participants in the 2004 Singlehanded Transpac Race—had dutifully printed out the National Weather Service's morning weather forecast before heading to our boats.

It was true. We would start our 2200-mile race from San Francisco Bay to Hanalei Bay in Kauai, Hawaii in gale force—twenty-five to forty mile per hour—winds. The first few days offshore comprise the roughest part of the passage between San Francisco and Hawaii. During that time, beating into the wind, the boat pounds into the waves. In ideal weather—ten to fifteeen knots of wind—it is an unpleasant beat. In a gale, it would be much worse.

But there was nothing to be done about the weather. The race was scheduled to start at ten a.m. on June 26 and the Race Committee had no intention of delaying it. We pulled on full foul weather gear, ready to confront the elements.

Each of the twenty-four skippers at the start had been preparing for this race for months. To meet the stringent race requirements, every one of us had upgraded electronics, sails, communications and safety equipment to pass inspection by the Race Committee. The race sponsor, the Singlehanded Sailing Society, had conducted monthly seminars since December 2003 to prepare potential participants. Local experts lectured on medical emergencies, sleep deprivation, food provisioning, sail choice and repair, emergency rudders, radios and telephones, route strategy, and arrival in Hanalei.

Even though I had sailed my family's boat, a Bristol 34 named Islander, twice across the Atlantic Ocean, I had made numerous purchases and improvements to qualify her for the race. But whatever I had done was done and whatever I had left undone would be up to me to improvise. After the start, all I would have available was what I had put on board.

The Singlehanded Transpac Race has been run every even-numbered year since 1978. Over two hundred sailors have competed in fourteen races. Of those, I was the tenth woman to make it to the start line and the only woman entrant in 2004. When asked, "Why do you want to do it?" my short answer was, "It's something I've wanted to do for years and now I'm ready." But why did I want to sail alone for days on end? Ever since reading Josiah Slocum's *Sailing Alone Around the World* as a teenager, I had dreamed of what it would be like to take off on a solo passage alone at the helm. My idol, Sir Francis Chichester, at age 62, sailed his Gypsy Moth II around the world. To me, sailing alone seemed like the ultimate adventure. I would be the only one responsible for my movement across the ocean from start to finish. I needed to see if I could actually do it on my own, without the assistance of crew. An added benefit, no one would be able to criticize whatever mistakes I made. I

~ On Board ~

did not see myself confronting the elements. Instead, with grace, the elements might permit me to pass through their undisputed domain. At age fifty-five, I wanted to make the attempt while still feeling young and strong. Having accumulated several thousand miles of offshore experience and hundreds of miles sailing alone, I was anxious to try.

The Race Committee had wired and sealed each boat's propeller shaft. Thus, we could not use our engines to propel us towards the finish, though we could still run our engines to refill batteries to provide power for instruments and lights. To get to the start line, beginning at 8:30 a.m., the Race Committee towed each boat out into Raccoon Straits, where we raised our sails and milled about, waiting for the gun.

Pow! A stream of boats flowed past the start. We headed for the Golden Gate Bridge, the first marker on our way. After that, in my mind, the second marker was Mile Rock; the third was getting through the shipping lines. Then there was nothing but open ocean to the Hawaiian Islands.

By afternoon, I had sailed out of sight of the coast. I sighed with relief. My worst fear is running into something. Once well away from land, I breathed easier. I prefer sailing surrounded by deep water on all sides. I feel much safer: my boat is a small island of security. I trust Islander. She was built in 1975 by Bristol; designed by Halsey Herreshoff to sail offshore. Her hull is thick and strong. She weighs a lot, one reason I was rated second slowest boat in our fleet.

It took all day to sail beyond the shipping lanes. The Monitor, a wind vane self-steering system, was at the helm, keeping Islander on course in relation to the relentless wind. Condensation inside my foulies made me cold and damp.

The boat pounding in the choppy seas made me violently seasick for the first time in my life. Then, as the gray skies darkened at the end of the afternoon, I saw that my jib was coming unstitched along its base. About three feet of binding flapped crazily. I pulled the jib in on its roller furler to keep the damage from getting worse. The rough seas prevented me from hauling it down and replacing it with my working jib. I continued sailing under main alone: progress slowed, Islander wallowing in the waves.

By law, ships must maintain a constant watch. Sailing alone, that is physically impossible. To me, "standing watch" meant that every twenty minutes I checked to make sure the wind was still blowing in the same direction, the main sail was trimmed and that there were no ships on the horizon. Night closed in. Too sick and exhausted to take off my foul weather gear and put it on again repeatedly, I spent the night fully dressed, leaning back next to the chart table, my feet propped on the companionway stairs. I pulled a Dacron comforter over my legs, set the egg timer for twenty minutes and tried to sleep. Each time it shrilled, I opened the hatch, climbed up to the cockpit, checked the compass and main sail and looked around 360 degrees for ships. Then I dropped down below. And set the egg timer again.

At one a.m., the wind shifted. I clipped in to my tether and carefully climbed to the aft of the cockpit. The Monitor likes to be adjusted in small increments. Turning the wheel that rotated the Monitor's vane, I gradually worked us back on course.

The twenty-minute increments became a blur of dozing and waking just enough to make a quick check, then falling back into a shallow sleep. At 3:20 a.m., I pulled myself up for a quick look around, looked, then looked again. Yes, there was a ship off to port. I could see the bright lights of the bridge, but couldn't make out a colored light—red for port or green for starboard—to tell me which way it was headed. I ducked below to grab binoculars. The compass in the binos allowed me to check the bearing of the ship. I huddled next to the dodger for the limited protection it offered from the wind. In five minutes, I checked the ship's bearing again. It seemed to have changed. That meant we were not on a collision course. But I checked again and again to make sure.

By morning, I was exhausted. I had survived the first night and all I wanted was to sleep. But I couldn't. Roll call started at nine a.m. Just before nine, I checked the GPS and wrote my coordinates in Islander's logbook. According to our communications plan, everyone would tune in to a specific channel on their single sideband radios. Rob McFarlane on Tigerbeetle emceed.

On Sunday, June 27, Rob opened roll call and asked if Dogbark copied. Al on Dogbark responded, "This is Dogbark. This is Dogbark." He recited his latitude, longitude, boat speed, direction and distance to finish. Rob repeated it then said, "I spoke with Ryan on his satellite phone" and gave Surfinn's position. "Rusalka, Rusalka, are you there?" Eric responded with his coordinates in the prescribed order. Rob worked his way through the list of twenty-four boats. The boats were listed by division and by handicap within their divisions. Islander was next to last. Rob called Islander and I tried to respond. But when I spoke into the microphone, the radio dial said "Hi SWR." I repeated my message over and over, but it went nowhere. My radio, which had transmitted clearly at the dock twenty-four hours before, was not working. After several calls to Islander, Rob gave up and moved on to Haulback.

At the end of roll call, Rob asked if anyone needed clarifications on any positions. Several boats asked him to repeat latitude or longitude of various boats. As he did so, each one of us, alone at our chart tables, was noting our competitors' coordinates. I had created a separate sheet for every roll call with blanks I could fill in as the positions were given. But that first morning, I was so sick to my stomach and bleary with fatigue I didn't even look at my roll sheets. Then Rob opened the radio meeting to conversation. I hung on to every word I could understand. Not everyone's radio transmitted with the same clarity. Only mine did not transmit at all.

I had a problem. I needed to let the Race Committee—and my family—know where I was. Greg Nelson, Commodore of the Singlehanded Sailing Society, on Starbuck, had already dropped out of the race because of ripped sails. Wen Lin—diabetic—on Wenlemir, was so seasick he couldn't keep down any food: a life-threatening situation. Alan Hebert, on Wisdom, reported "oil-canning" problems with his hull. By contrast, I was not in any difficulty—and I definitely didn't want anyone to worry about me.

When I purchased it in 1999, my back-up communications system was cutting-edge technology. Now the GSC—Global Satellite Communications—was nearly passé. Happily, I had reactivated it. I sent a short email to my husband Dean and Rich Ray, Chairman of the Race Committee, giving my position and confirming that I was safe, though seasick. Dean had promised to forward my messages to our two daughters and other family and friends. The GSC carries it messages using a limited number of satellites. I pushed "Send." My unit showed the message in queue. When a satellite from the system passed overhead, my machine would transmit the message. That didn't happen until three p.m. that afternoon. Finally, the message flew from my machine to a satellite. When the satellite passed over a ground station, it downloaded my message. From there, the ground station sent the message to Dean's and Ray's computers.

At six p.m., I tuned in the to the weather broadcast. Don Anderson, an accomplished amateur forecaster, had volunteered to give our fleet a daily update on the location of the Pacific high. His broadcast came through loud and clear. The location of the high would help us determine our routes to Hawaii. In choosing a route, one's type of boat mattered. Lighter boats could afford to sail extra miles in pursuit of the best wind. Heavier boats, like mine, traditionally stuck close to the rhumb line, the shortest distance between the start and finish. After giving the weather, Don asked for comments or questions. Mark Deppe of Achera announced that when he emailed everyone's position to Rich Ray, Rich replied that he had received an email from Islander. Relief washed over me. Messages had flown back and forth across the water and folks knew where I was. Invisible waves connected me to family and friends.

The wind remained strong. The relatively relaxed day darkened into night. Well beyond the shipping lanes, I extended my sleeping time to thirty minutes between checks. Even at that, it was misery. At three a.m., the wind had shifted about thirty degrees. As I scrunched down in the cockpit, it gusted to thirty-two knots. Fighting the wind, I adjusted the Monitor onto course and Islander's motion gradually smoothed. There were no stars in the cloud-filled sky. No time to sit outside and dream. I eased myself below and reset the egg timer.

Next morning, as Rob worked his way through the nine a.m. roll call, I filled in the blanks giving each boat's location. When Rob got to Islander, he said, "Good morning, Islander. We know you are out there and wish you a very good day." Surrounded by infinite gray sky and dark waves, my eyes filled with tears.

Days assumed shape: twenty-four hours divided into three-hour increments. Nine a.m. roll call, six p.m. weather and nine p.m. roll call highlights; log entries noon, three, six, nine p.m., midnight, three, six, nine a.m., noon. Nights were infinitely harder than days. I woke up each half hour to check all around. During the day, figuring Islander was visible, I allowed myself up to three-hour naps.

On Tuesday, June 29, I ventured onto the foredeck with my storm jib. As soon as I set it, Islander's balance improved. The sun came out. With thirteen knots of wind, Islander rocked along making over six knots under a partly cloudy blue sky. I opened up the hatch to dry below decks; solar panels recharged the batteries. Relaxing, I began to enjoy the passage.

Next day, I dropped the storm jib. I pulled the damaged jib off the roller furler and replaced it with an eighty-five percent jib—the working jib I had brought to use when running downwind. To keep from creating a mess of lines, or making a potentially dangerous mistake, I moved slowly and deliberately. Before I tackled any project, I thought it through step by step, movement by movement. Chronically fatigued, operating at considerably less than one hundred percent, I spent hours changing each sail. Once I raised the working jib, I shook the reef out of the main. Then the wind dropped to seven knots. Two days after a gale, I wished with all my heart for more wind.

That night, after listening to Don's evening weather report, I heated a quart of fresh water and took a sponge bath. I pulled on clean clothes. How civilized! I stretched out on the settee and for hours read one of Patrick O'Brian's seafaring adventures—punctuated each thirty minutes by a check outside.

Measuring the days in miles from the Corinthian Yacht Club, miles remaining to Hanalei Bay, I passed the one-quarter mark on July 1. Chronically preoccupied with my speed, I feared arriving in Hanalei after the official end of the race and being classified "DNF": Did Not Finish. Rich Ray had emailed, reminding me that providing my whereabouts by email did not constitute "checking in" as required by the sailing instructions. I was being penalized one hour for each day I did not check in. In order to arrive within the twenty-one day duration of the race, I had to average five knots—five nautical miles per hour—for every hour of every day. Considering my accumulating penalty, I needed to average even better than that. Each day, the rest of the fleet stretched further ahead of me. As Dean pointed out before the race, I had never averaged five knots on any previous passage. This time I prayed would be different.

On July 4, eight days after the start, I reached the trade winds. At last I could set twin jibs to sail downwind. Attaching my spinnaker pole to the working jib and poling it out to starboard, I lifted the pole on its topping lift. A foreguy attached to the lower bridle kept it from going too high.

Next I set the storm jib and pulled it out to port. The main was also flying to port, covering the storm jib. However, the storm jib created a flow of air in front of the main, pulling the boat forward. This was not the twin sail arrangement I had envisioned. In fact, these twins were so small, they looked silly. But until I figured out how to repair my larger jib, I was flying all the sail I had.

Hooking up the electric self-steering allowed me to sail nearly directly downwind. My Wheelpilot 5000 wouldn't start, but my older, smaller Autohelm 3000 connected right away. That evening, the wind picked up considerably. Double-reefing the main, I left the twin headsails flying. With twenty knots of wind, the Autohelm could not keep Islander on course. I set up the Monitor and headed up into the wind just enough so the Monitor would work.

Day by day, the weather grew warmer. I traded foul weather gear for shorts and a tank top. The non-skid deck covering, a tan-colored material that absorbs heat, burned my bare feet. Wary of sunburn, I slathered myself with suntan lotion and wore a safari hat with a neck curtain. I looked ridiculous—and didn't care one bit.

I spent hours in the cockpit, Islander's living room. The view extends to the horizon in all directions. This huge living space changes constantly. Dramatic colors and cloud patterns herald sunrise and sunset like theatrically-staged events. On the horizontal plane, the swell throbs like the ocean's heartbeat. During dark, stormy days I hid below to avoid the endless whitecaps. On calm, sunny days, I sat outside and marveled at the immensity.

On previous passages, I spent watches in the cockpit. Sailing solo, I kept watch differently. Desperately trying to reduce my sleep deficit, I spent much more time below decks napping. And so, though sometimes I thought I heard the whoosh of whale or the sigh of a dolphin, I missed seeing those that must have passed.

Eleven days out, on July 7, a white spinnaker billowed up over the horizon. The Pac Cup Race from San Francisco Bay to Oahu had started the week after the Singlehanded Transpac. These larger, fully-crewed boats would pass through our fleet. This was the first sailboat I had seen since leaving San Francisco. At last, I had an opportunity to speak with someone. My VHF radio operates only for short line-of-sight distances. For fifteen minutes, I tried to raise the white-sailed boat. Why wouldn't it respond? At last, the captain answered. Icon was indeed competing in the Pac Cup. Excitedly, I explained I had spoken to no one since leaving San Francisco and asked him to contact the Singlehanded Transpac Race Committee to confirm Islander's location. The captain was not inclined to chat. He could not have realized what that short conversation meant to me.

Two days later, on July 9, I painstakingly repaired the jib. Using an awl to make holes in the stiff, reinforced foot of the sail, I pulled whipping cord through the holes and tied the ends together. I tacked it together at four locations; enough, I hoped, to keep it together for the final 700 miles.

Time to move sails around. First, I brought in the storm jib. Then I dropped the working jib and tied it to the lifeline with a bungee cord. I hauled the large jib onto the foredeck and raised it, sliding it into the groove of the roller furler. Finally, I poled it out. Then I raised the working jib on the spinnaker halyard, using the other groove of the roller furler. Immediately, boat speed increased by a knot. For the first time during the passage, I had the sails in the positions I had planned. I headed for the finish line, full speed ahead.

The fastest boats in the fleet were crossing the finish line, one or more a day, while I was a week behind. Tigerbeetle finished and Bill Merrick on Ergo took over roll call. Ergo's signal had never come through as well Tigerbeetle's. I couldn't hear roll call any more at all. Those friendly words had given me a sense of belonging. I deeply missed my daily greetings from the fleet.

On top of that, emails were not leaving my GSC. Faithfully, every twelve hours I wrote an email giving my position and a couple of sentences about the day's events. The emails stacked up in my out box. It seemed like a personal failing. My mother, in particular, was worried about my sailing alone. I didn't want her to suffer. I felt miserable and, for the first time, terribly alone. Rationally, I knew it was all a matter of satellite coverage of the area—obviously incomplete. I had been physically alone since I crossed the start line, but I had had a sense of being connected. Even though I hadn't spoken, except for the brief exchange with Icon, I had been able to communicate. Now I was isolated. I felt more vulnerable than I had since sailing out into the opening gale. If anything happened to me, how would I let someone know?

At noon on July 12, 450 miles from the finish line, twin headsails flying, I was down below when a terrific gust of wind shook the boat. I heard a loud crash and raced outside. The large jib had back winded and bent the pole at right angles. In a flash, I realized there was no way to repair it: my down wind sail was over.

In mourning, I unhooked the ruined pole and clipped it to the lifeline stantions. I dropped the working jib and carried it back to the cockpit. The finish line had seemed so close. Now—forced to sail on a broad reach with much less sail area—it had receded dramatically. During the down wind days, I had felt fairly confident I could arrive before the official end of the race at midnight on July 17. With this latest setback, I was no longer so sure.

On July 14, a satellite picked up one of the emails that had been sitting in my out box for days. Hopefully whenever Dean received it, it would relieve my family's fears. I wished I could hear from them. I hadn't received an email since July 8. Although I had to believe people were trying to contact me, my mailbox consistently said "Empty." In frustration with the single side band radio, I had given up trying to pick up roll call. I was getting very tired of being completely alone.

The wind blew directly towards Hanalei Bay, but I was forced to sail in long zigzags to approach the finish. I sailed west until I crossed the rhumb line, then headed south. By heading south, I could pass close to Oahu before turning west to Kauai. As the sun rose on July 15, I searched the horizon for a dim outline of land. There it was! The mountains of Oahu rose like blue shadows from the waves. Mentally, I cheered.

At 2:30 a.m., in the early morning dark, I had double-reefed the main. Now I was glad I had. With twenty-two knots of wind, I gybed and skimmed west along the coast of Oahu towards my final goal. Using my VHF radio, I called the Coast Guard on Oahu to request communications assistance. The friendly voice agreed to contact Dean and the

Race Committee with my coordinates. Talking with someone infused me with a burst of strength and enthusiasm: less than one hundred miles to go.

The sailing instructions suggested racers start calling the Race Committee by VHF radio from about seventy-five miles out. As soon as I reached that point, I commenced calling. I expected to arrive at the finish line in the middle of the night and wanted to make sure the Race Committee would guide me into reef-protected Hanalei Bay. In the distance, I could see the blue silhouette of Kauai; then, as it got dark, the island disappeared into a bank of clouds. I headed to a point north of the island, searching for the Kilalei Point light to guide me in.

At midnight, I still had not raised the Race Committee by VHF. After all these days at sea, would I end up crashing on the reef? Feeling very nervous, I contemplated turning back out to sea until daylight.

The only other piece of communications equipment I had on board was my cell phone. The Race Committee had monitored its satellite phone as long as other boats were out there. But the last boat had arrived at least two days ago —and the Race Committee knew I did not have a satellite phone. Desperately, I dialed. A phone rang and rang. "Hello, Race Committee? This is Barbara Euser on Islander." "Barbara, this is Dean." I nearly dropped the phone.

Dean had arrived on Kauai that afternoon. He woke the Race Committee and I communicated with them by VHF. Folks drove to the Bay, jumped into a motorized skiff and headed out to meet me. Once the Committee member at headquarters confirmed that I had crossed the finish line— forty-five hours before the end of the race—the skiff pulled

~ On Board ~

alongside. Five men scrambled aboard: Rich and Bill of the Race Committee, Greg, Commodore of the Singlehanded Sailing Society who himself had dropped out of the race on day two, Louis, owner of the skiff, and Dean.

Rich took the helm and instructed me to take a seat and relax; the Race Committee would take it from there. This was the same reception each of the other boats had received upon crossing the finish line: relief at the helm, escort into the Bay. Once the wires immobilizing the prop shaft had been cut, motor started, jib furled in and anchor attached to its rode, all six of us assembled in the cockpit. Bill lifted his backpack to his lap and pulled out a bottle of champagne. He poured it into plastic glasses and proposed a toast: "Congratulations to the first woman to finish the Singlehanded Transpac 2004!"

Lurley and the Singlehanded TransPac
~

I was scheduled to sail the Singlehanded TransPac, a solo race from San Francisco to Hawaii, when I first saw *Lurley* and fell in love with her.

Getting ready for the Singlehanded TransPac was a matter of life and death. Sponsored by the Singlehanded Sailing Society, monthly seminars for those planning to sail the 2004 race began in December 2003. At the first seminar I was awed by sailors planning to sail their second or third solo race. I was one of a handful of neophytes, the only woman. I needed to absorb as much information as I could from every seminar. I needed every bit of help I could get.

In the midst of these early preparations for the race, in early January 2004, I traveled to Europe on business. While in Paris, I surfed my favorite topic on the web: Canal Boats Europe. One site that came up was comprised of yachts for sale by British owners. Scrolling through, I found two boats that greatly appealed to me. One was in Britain, as were most all the boats on that site. The other was in France—Southern France, Le Segala on the Canal du Midi.

She was described as a gentleman's motor yacht, steel hull, graceful lines, place for seven to sleep. The photo looked like the boat I had been dreaming of for years. I e-mailed the yacht company asking for contact with the owner. The next day I received a reply, including a phone number. I called. The British owners were selling their beloved *Lurley* because Peter had grown too old to take care of her anymore. He and Caroline wanted to buy a house of their own in southern France and selling *Lurley* offered the way.

I needed to go see this boat. There are thousands of boats for sale at any given moment. But boats are not fungible. Each has her own characteristics and personality. I had looked at hundreds of boats on websites over the past seven years and had never fallen in love before.

From Paris it is a five-hour ride on the fast train to Toulouse. Then there is a short train ride to Castelnaudary. I had asked Caroline how I would recognize her and Peter. She said to look for a woman with bright red hair and a man with a full white beard. I saw them immediately.

Caroline drove us to Le Segala where *Lurley* was docked in front of their house. They shared the house with another couple, Caroline and Peter splitting their own time between the house and summers on the Canal du Midi on *Lurley*. They showed me through the boat and Peter gave me a thorough introduction to the two engines. Then we went inside the house for lunch. After lunch, Caroline drove me to Toulouse to catch the train back to Paris. I spent the entire ride back trying to figure out how to buy *Lurley*. I thought that if I could find another couple to join as partners in buying *Lurley*, it might be possible. When I got back to Paris, I e-mailed Caroline and Peter, told them how much I hoped I would be able to find a way to buy *Lurley*. It wasn't clear.

But I had other things on my mind. The Singlehanded TransPac was coming up at the end of June. Even though I had paid my entry fee, I couldn't start the race until I had completed my qualifying sail: a four-hundred-mile long solo sail at least one hundred miles offshore. And before I could do that, I had a lot of preparation to do. I began by taking *Islander* out for short sails alone on San Francisco Bay. I would go out for a couple of hours. Just leaving the dock alone, motoring out to where I could raise the main sail and sailing the boat all by myself required new skills. I learned a lot, quickly. Then I had to venture out the Gate, that is, sail under the Golden Gate Bridge into the Pacific Ocean. I love to sail under that massive bridge and feel the heartbeat of the ocean, the ocean swell. Sailing under it alone was another matter.

One day, I sailed out to the Lightship, more accurately known as the San Francisco Buoy, about fourteen miles offshore. At Easter, I entered the Singlehanded Farallones Race, a race around a group of islands twenty-eight miles out. The Bay was shrouded in dense fog as I crossed the start line and sailed under the Gate. Halfway to the Lightship, the wind died. One by one, racers abandoned the race. Finally, I radioed the Race Committee, turned on my engine and motored home.

I needed to get closer to the Farallones. After all, if I couldn't get to the Farallones, how could I sail over two thousand miles to Hawaii? One week later, I had my chance. In clear weather, I made the sail.

Then I needed to spend one night at sea on my own. So I planned an overnight sail. I started in the afternoon and only went as far as the area south of the Farallones, between

~ On Board ~

the southbound and westbound shipping lanes. During the night, the wind died. I floated uncomfortably, my sails hanging, rigging clanging. Every ten minutes I got up to check all around for boat traffic, then dropped back to sleep. By the time morning came, I was an exhausted wreck. But I had spent my first night alone at sea.

The final hurdle to entering the race was my qualifying sail. I couldn't wait until the last minute to do it. The weather could deteriorate. I might not make it on my first attempt. I wanted to minimize the pressure as much as I could. I prepared the boat, bought provisions—then waited for a window of good weather. Finally at the end of May, I had it: the five-day forecast was for moderate winds and moderate seas. The first night was horrible. Getting up every ten minutes was a rhythm I could not sustain—even for four nights. The next night I was past my required limit of one hundred miles offshore. I turned and sailed north. I got up every twenty minutes and felt marginally better the next morning. I spent four nights at sea. When I returned to Richmond Yacht Club, completing my qualifying sail, I understood why it was a requirement. I had demonstrated to myself that I could sail all the way to Hawaii.

In the midst of my preparations for the Singlehanded TransPac, I was pursuing different alternatives for financing the purchase of *Lurley*. There were not many people I would feel comfortable sharing my boat with. Then a friend, who is also a financial expert, came up with a creative solution.

Excitedly, I e-mailed Caroline and Peter. I was worried *Lurley* might have already been sold. She had not. In a flurry of transatlantic e-mails and a wire transfer, the deed was done. *Lurley* belonged to my husband and me. I flew to Paris, took the train to Toulouse. This time I was not just checking on a boat, I was taking possession of *Lurley*.

Caroline and Peter had taken a last cruise from Le Segala to Toulouse and installed her at her new home in the Toulouse marina, Port Saint Sauveur. Caroline and Peter met me at the station and drove me to the marina. They had *Lurley* in sparkling condition. Midday in June, the port was hot. We boarded *Lurley* and, with Peter at the helm, motored up the canal to a shady spot. Caroline stepped onto the grassy bank and expertly drove in two stakes and we tied up. We ate lunch aboard on the calm canal in the shade of venerable plane trees and talked about *Lurley*. Then Peter asked me to take the helm. I drove us to the first lock, then handed the controls to Peter. He and Caroline showed me how it is done.

We dropped Caroline at the small wooden fishing pier before the lock. She walked to the lock keeper's, carrying a ball of blue cord with a large stainless steel hook on the end. Peter drove us through the narrow lock entrance and we pulled over to the left side where Caroline had dropped the hook for us, fishing for the two mooring lines with loops tied at their ends. I placed the loops on the hook and she pulled it up. No tossing of lines, no fuss. Like artists, they made a difficult maneuver look easy.

Caroline ran the stern line around one of the mushroom-shaped bollards on the quay and dropped the line down to me. Then she walked with the bow line to another bollard, ran it around the bollard and pulled the line taut.

The lock keeper opened the gate and water rushed into the lock, floating us up to the next level of the canal. When the water inside the lock was level with the water outside

~ On Board ~

the lock, the lock keeper opened the lock gates, Caroline stabilized the boat while I pulled the lines in. Then with a small shove, she pushed the boat away from the side of the lock and stepped aboard. Peter maneuvered *Lurley* smoothly out of the lock into the canal.

Just above the lock, Peter pulled over. This time I jumped out and pounded in the stakes and tied *Lurley* to the bank. They spent another hour explaining *Lurley* and recounting their exploits in her over the years. After an interval they judged sufficient to keep the lock keeper from getting angry with us for wasting his time, I pulled up the stakes and Peter turned the boat around. It was my turn to take *Lurley* through a lock.

Very slowly and carefully, I lined *Lurley* up with the lock entrance. Slowly she moved into the lock. When we were alongside the quay, Caroline stepped onto the quay, ran the lines around the bollards and calmly stepped back aboard. She and Peter each took a line, while I stayed at the helm, tightly gripping the wheel.

At the bottom of the lock, I steered through the narrow opening into the seemingly broad canal. The longer I steered the boat, the less tightly I gripped the wheel. I had insisted on standing behind the wheel. After going under a couple of bridges, I relaxed enough to take my seat in the elevated captain's chair. I owned *Lurley* on paper, but it would take time and work and experience handling her to own her on the Canal.

When I got back to California, there were only two weeks to go until the race.

On June 26, the morning of the race, I printed out the weather map and forecast for San Francisco Bay to one hundred miles offshore. The word GALE featured prominently. Along the dock, racers joked, "Turn right at the A in GALE!" Dressed in full foul- weather gear, sails reefed, twenty-four sailors started. Within three days, three had dropped out due to problems with either health or equipment. For me, the first three days passed in a blur of sailing through heavy weather coupled with seasickness. At the first roll call, I discovered that, although I could hear the broadcast, my radio would not transmit. Using my handheld e-mail device, I communicated the difficulty to my husband Dean and the Race Committee. For the duration of the race, I e-mailed my position to my racing colleagues, but I did not speak with anyone.

By the fourth day, the weather improved. My stomach became accustomed to the motion of the waves. Days assumed a rhythm as I trimmed sails, adjusted the self-steering mechanism, charted my position, kept the log. I was free to enjoy the open expanse of the ocean.

I love sailing offshore. Out of sight of land, there are no pathways restricting movement. Surrounded completely by water, the choice is one's own. The race prescribed a destination, but each day offered a multitude of choices, dependent only on the direction of the wind.

In the middle of the ocean, my thoughts returned to *Lurley* and the Canal du Midi. Perhaps it is this contrast that gives *Lurley* most appeal. Compared to the open expanses of the ocean, the canal is at the opposite extreme. The canal is a narrow, man-made channel: no deviations allowed. A small boat in the wide ocean is essentially insecure; a boat in the canal is contained, enfolded within secure tree-lined banks. The ocean offers me the world. In *Islander*, I could sail anywhere. Ironically, that is also the appeal of the canals.

France boasts seven thousand kilometers of navigable waterways. Not all are as benign as the Canal du Midi. The Rhone, the main artery of France, is a forceful river, despite the gigantic locks that regulate its flow. The cities and countries of Europe are connected by waterways as well as by roads. I could take *Lurley* from Toulouse north to St. Petersburg or down the Danube to the Black Sea. Despite the contrast in watery milieu, *Islander* and *Lurley* are connected by the opportunities they afford for adventure and exploration.

Alone on *Islander*, it took me twenty days to reach Kauai. I was content in my solitude, but happy to reach the Islands and finish the race. Dean was there to meet me.

But that was only half the distance. Sailing to Hawaii is essentially a down-wind sail. Sailing back to San Francisco is harder and takes longer. I sailed back with a young woman named Mariah. Having just sailed to Hawaii by myself, I felt confident about my sailing abilities. But Mariah had a lot to teach me, and she did. The return sail took twenty-eight days. When we finally made it into *Islander*'s slip at Richmond Yacht Club, I was ready for a rest. Spending time on *Lurley* on the Canal du Midi never sounded more appealing.

In December, following a reading to celebrate publication of a new anthology, a group of writers retired to a nearby bar. The conversation turned to Europe, then France, then the South of France. I told about acquiring *Lurley*, berthed on the Canal du Midi.

"What a perfect place to write!" someone offered. I thought of the shady, tree-lined canal and violet-shuttered stucco houses, the fields of sunflowers. Looking around at the casually assembled writers, engaged in conversation, I felt a wave of affection.

"It would be fun to get a group of writers together," I said automatically. There were expressions of agreement, nodding of heads. "It could be workshop," someone offered. "We could publish a book," added a third. "It does sound like fun," I replied, and the conversation moved on.

The idea of a workshop took on a life of its own. How many people could *Lurley* hold? That would dictate how large the workshop could be. Who would the instructor be? Would there be one or several? If one were to publish an anthology, how many essays would be required? Who would the writers be? I had done some of these things before. In 2002, I had published an anthology of garden essays called *Bay Area Gardening*. The book included sixty-four short essays. A book of travel essays would contain longer essays, but the concept was the same. In 2002, I had been working as the director of a non-profit writers organization and organized writing seminars and hired writing instructors. The more I thought about it, the more feasible it seemed. I contacted a friend and fellow-writer with experience in publicity. She thought the idea sounded good—in fact, she would like to go on a seminar herself—and agreed to publicize it. But publicize what exactly? The idea was still forming. A series of one-week workshops, with different instructors, sounded like a good way to organize the writing sessions. I contacted several friends who were writing instructors to test the idea. Each one I spoke to agreed to teach. Finding teachers was obviously not the challenge. Finding writers

~ On Board ~

was. With a scant six months before the workshops would take place, we began to spread the word.

Writers, friends of mine, were all pressed for time. Pushed by deadlines and the constant press of the details of life, we all lead harried lives. On the Canal du Midi, I had discovered the antidote and I wanted to share it. We would slow down, enjoy the serenity of the canal, have time to reflect and write about whatever we encountered along our way. A select group of writers decided to take the voyage.

Chez Paul
~

We were having our breakfast coffee and croissants under the red and white-striped awning of Chez Paul, a small rural bar on the Canal du Midi. Madame, the proprietor's wife, arrived with a piece of fabric, actually two pieces of fabric, one red and one black, sewn together. She stood at the pool table in the center of the room and carefully cut the fabric in strips, creating half-red, half-black ribbons. Then she began festooning the bar. We asked why.

Madame looked amazed. *"Vous ne savez pas?* (You don't know?)" That afternoon, she explained, the World Cup Rugby Championship game would be played in Scotland. The teams vying for World Champion were the local Stade Toulousain and Stade France, the Paris team.

She pointed to an old photograph on the wall. *"Ça c'est un stade rugby. C'est mon mari."* She pointed first to the fit, handsome young man in the photo, then to Paul, her husband, still trim and relatively fit but with a shock of white hair, behind the bar. Full-color posters of the Stade Toulousain lineup covered the pool table. When we left, Madame offered us one.

~ *On Board* ~

Dean and I took our boat *Lurley* for an excursion further along the canal. At the lock called Negra, we stopped for lunch and walked up the hill to Montesquieu-Lauragais. After coffee at the only restaurant in town, we worked our way back through the locks to our comfortable mooring of the night before.

As we approached Chez Paul, shouts rang out. "*Merde! Goal Stade France!*" The wrong team had just scored a goal. We tied Lurley up to the canal bank and hurried to watch the match. The atmosphere in the bar was tense. Eyes riveted to the television set hanging from the ceiling in the corner took no notice as Dean and I squeezed our way inside.

Trying our best to be invisible—to avoid blocking anyone's view—we maneuvered ourselves to the bar. Only the bartender stood behind us, and he had space enough for a clear view of the game. Just one barstool was available. The only other seat not occupied was covered by a coat, abandoned by its owner, who was engrossed in the game. The bartender, Paul himself, saw our dilemma, reached for the coat, stuffed it behind the counter and took our order. Without taking his eyes off the game, he poured our drinks and pushed them our way.

We were trying to figure out how this all-engrossing game of rugby might be scored, when a wave of expressions of disgust rolled through the crowd. A player from Stade Toulousain had blown a chance to score.

Chez Paul had been empty at breakfast. That afternoon, it was packed. The pool table had been moved into the corner. Seven of the bar's ten tables had been stacked on top of it. Only one group sat at a table—the remaining three tables pushed into one. The rest of the room was standing room only.

A full commentary blared from the television. An even fuller commentary was conducted by rugby pundits in the bar, first from one side of the room, then another.

We reached for a half-empty plate of peanuts.

Only one man in the room wore a suit and tie. He pushed back from the table where he held the patriarchal position and worked his way to the bar. Another round of drinks for his table, he ordered. He examined us intently, then asked which team we were for. "Toulouse!" Dean and I exclaimed. "Where are you from?" he demanded. I told him we were Americans, but we kept our boat in Toulouse, so we were partly from Toulouse. That was the right answer. He motioned to Paul to fill up our glasses.

Then he explained the reason this rugby match was so important: Stade Toulousain was playing against Stade France. Toulouse was not a part of France, he said. Toulouse had never really been a part of France. After the Albigensian Crusade [in the early 1200s], the French kings from the north had claimed Toulouse, but Toulouse was still not part of France. Today's match would show the victor.

There was more riding on this match than we had supposed.

The ball moved up and down the field. First one team formed a scrum, then the other. The first half was almost over. Stade France was up one goal. Then Stade Toulousain seized an opportunity and scored. We all cheered loudly. At the half, the score was tied.

Halftime offered an opportunity for everyone to order another drink. Once again our glasses were refilled. This

~ *On Board* ~

time it was a man of Middle Eastern demeanor who welcomed us to root for Stade Toulousain. And we truly did. A huge mound of peanuts appeared on our plate.

It crossed my mind briefly that, not far away, Toulon and several other cities had elected mayors from the Front National, the party of Jean-Marie Le Pen, which opposes any immigration, especially from Islamist countries, into France. But that didn't mar this patron's enthusiasm—or ours.

Stade Toulousain was playing as though their lives depended on the outcome of this match, as though it actually was part of the centuries' old division between north and south. And Stade Toulousain scored again! The bar erupted in shouts and clapping. We were up one goal.

The game was clearly not over yet. Stade France fought back. Every time they approached the goal, the bar quieted and people pulled in their breath. Waves of emotion surged across the room as the two teams waged battle on television. Dean and I were hoarse from shouting.

But this was Stade Toulousain's match. With one final goal, Stade Toulousain secured the World Cup and victory—for Toulouse, and, at least in Chez Paul, for the South of France.

CHAPTER FOUR

India, Ireland and Italy

Kerala with Two Girls in Tow

~

Like pink and yellow butterflies they edged along the road, an endless stream of women with silken saris fluttering in the breeze. We had just flown in Trivandrum, at the southern tip of India. As we left the airport baggage claim area, we were overwhelmed by the heat and smells and press of people. Our solid, square London taxicab was an island of peace parting the waves of humanity.

The narrow, winding road was the main artery between Trivandrum and points north. We were headed to the game preserve at Periyar, a national park in the Cardamom Hills region of the Western Ghats. But that was too far for one afternoon's drive.

I was sitting on the jump seat, facing backwards, so Dean, my husband, and two daughters, Helane, thirteen, and Piper, nine, could ride facing forward.

We had lived in Guangzhou, China for eighteen months when the girls were younger. At the time of our India trip, we were living in Paris. The previous Christmas, we had camped in the Sinai and snorkeled in the Red Sea. Yet despite our girls' travel experience, I was worried that life in India might be too harsh for them to witness. We chose to visit the southwestern state of Kerala because it is relatively middle-class and rural, and indeed, the people we passed along the road appeared healthy, dressed in adequate clothes. Nowhere did we see the terrible poverty that is found in cities like Calcutta.

Helane tends to get carsick, and the narrow, twisting road made her uncomfortable. The only solution was for her to keep focused on the scenery. The women's bright saris captivated her imagination. She asked about the red marks on their foreheads. Her own forehead was glued to the window.

At dusk, we arrived at our motel. As stated in our guidebook, the rooms were "simply furnished." Ours had white-washed concrete walls, a concrete floor, a bed and a cracked dresser. As we walked to the adjoining restaurant, large rats scurried across our path, disappearing into thick-grown weeds.

Table and chairs were set on a sparse lawn, overlooking a small lake. Strings of colored lights gave the modest restaurant a festive air. We were ravenous after the long drive, and the food surpassed our expectations. We had never tasted more delicate spring rolls. Shrimp and vegetable curries were rich with flavor, not overly spicy. The combination of Chinese and Indian choices on the menu surprised us, but were soon came to understand that this coast is home to many cultures melded together. Dessert was bananas, sweet-coated, deep-fried, and mellow. Well-satisfied, we returned to our rooms.

In seconds, Helane telephoned from the girls' room. Come quick! A gigantic bug! Dean and I rushed in to find a six-inch-long cockroach lumbering confidently across the floor. Dean took off his shoe and beat it. He scooped it up with a sheet of paper and deposited it outside. Only slightly stunned, the cockroach quickly recovered and resumed his stroll, now along the sidewalk. Slightly shaken ourselves, we assured the girls they would be fine if they kept their feet off the floor. They clung to each other for safety.

When Dean and I returned to our room, we noticed, just above the headboard of our bed, a half-inch wide line of ants marching resolutely across the wall. We moved the bed across the room and fell into a deep sleep. By morning, the ants had completed their crossing.

I reflected on how much closer the relationship between humans and animals—in this case, vermin and insects—was in India than at home. Our solid apartment building kept rats confined to the basement. And in France we simply did not have insects as intimidating as those in the tropics. I thought of the mothers and children of India, of their everyday relationship with these beings. Living close to the earth means living as neighbors, possibly housemates, with disease-carrying rats and roaches.

In the bright morning light, the cockroach incident seemed funny. The rats stayed hidden in the weeds. The marshy shores of the lake were alive with herons and egrets. The restaurant's plastic tables and chairs seemed less romantic by daylight, but we nonetheless enjoyed our black tea with milk and sugar and toasted bread. A taxi and driver soon arrived and we headed toward the game preserve of Periyar.

We drove for hours, passing through farm fields and one small town after another. The driver slowed for the white, wide-horned sacred cows that wandered across town streets, sampling the merchandise from fruit vendors' stands.

Late afternoon, we arrived at the main lodge in Periyar. It gave the impression of a colonial hunting lodge, built with sturdy timbers and stone, a wide veranda stretching along three sides. Tourists stood on the balcony with binoculars, looking for monkeys, elephants or tigers.

Our guide arrived the next morning at eight o'clock, walking through the thick vegetation in rubber sandals, carrying a stout walking stick. He walked lightly, as though unwilling to disturb grass and bushes. Despite the heat, we'd been told to wear long pants, long sleeves and athletic shoes for protection against insects and skin-irritating plants. We carried water and lunch in a daypack.

The first animals we saw were monkeys, who simultaneously ignored us and seemed to perform for our benefit. Dozens of skinny brown animals tripped lightly along the branches overhead, chattering constantly. The girls were riveted.

Our guide led us over logs across marshy terrain then along the edge of a small lake, one of a series of waterways in Periyar. Wildlife convenes on the reedy banks. Our guide was endlessly turning his head, watching and listening for signs of animals that we would never have picked up. Silently, he pointed ahead. One the far side of an inlet, six wild boar crashed out of the bush, splashing through the water as they rushed headlong from whatever pursued them.

There are tigers in Periyar. I half-hoped we would see one. But I was satisfied to hike all day through changing micro-climates. One moment we were sloshing alongside a lake, then climbing up a desert-like hillside. Then back under the cover of trees.

~ India, Ireland and Italy ~

Our guide walked slowly, setting a measured pace. He was attuned to his charges for the day. He offered a rest stop in a grove of trees with branches low enough to climb on. The girls clambered along the broad branches, unwittingly imitating the monkeys we had seen. Piper swung on a long thick vine, Helane pushing her as though it were a swing: Tarzan clichés. But in a jungle, swinging on a vine is the obvious thing to do.

Once again close to the lake, we could hear splashing. Elephants, legs like columns, rose out of the shallow water. With their trunks, they splashed themselves and sprayed their youngsters.

By afternoon, we began to recognize some forest we had seen before. The long loop of our day's hike was nearly over. The girls had hiked all day without complaint. The constantly changing environments and intermittent animals had kept them focused—no time to get tired.

The next day, we took a taxi to a nearby town to explore and shop. Along the street and in the shops, everyone seemed fascinated by Piper's blond hair, blue eyes and pale skin. Women did not hesitate to touch her hair and pat her arm.

We visited spice shops, sniffing and purchasing fresh ground spices. We found a store that sold stick-on *bindis*. Helane purchased a packet and the shopkeeper applied the "third eye of wisdom" to her forehead. Another store was stacked with silk scarves and baggy silk pants in every color. We couldn't resist buying for ourselves and gifts for friends. Finally, we entere a fabric store. The shop girl held up one bolt after another, draping Piper and Helane in shimmering colors. We emerged laden with bags of rich brocades.

Back at Periyar, after a short nap, we boarded a tourist boat for a sunset ride along the park's waterways. We struck up a conversation with a family from New Delhi. The older daughter was about the same age as Helane. Speaking British-accented English, she told Helane about her school. She went to an all-girls' school. Did Helane? At her school, they wore uniforms. Did Helane wear a uniform to school? I heard her ask what kind of money we use in America. I saw Helane pull a dollar out of her bag, which the girl rubbed slowly between her fingers. They drifted slowly down the railing, out of parental earshot.

The animals were coming to the water to drink. They lifted their heads at the sound of the boat's motor, then resumed drinking. In one cove, we saw antelope. In another, elephants. Flocks of birds flew by, then plunged into the water, fishing. An eagle perched on a channel marker.

As the sun sank, the sky turned to flames. Small gray cloud puffs paraded in front of the inferno. Our small boat chugged back to the lodge as stars appeared.

After dinner, Helane complained her stomach hurt. Then in a quick rush to our bathroom, she vomited. What had she eaten? We decided Piper would stay in our room with Dean, and I would spend the night in the girls' room with Helane. It was a sleepless night for Helane and me.

Anticipating a long night, Dean had handed me a copy of *The Shipping News* by Annie Proulx. Settling into bed, I started reading. Before the end of the first chapter, Helane was throwing up again, me beside her. We spent most of the night in the large bathroom. I sat with my back against the white tile walls. Helane was curled on a towel on the hard tile floor, in between violent vomiting episodes. For me, *The Shipping News* proved a riveting tale. By the time the sky was getting light and Helane's stomach stopped spasming, I finished the book—now forever linked in my mind with white tile and Periyar.

For breakfast, Helane drank weak tea. She declared she had just experienced the most miserable night of her life. Fortunately, she had eliminated whatever had poisoned her system.

Our plan for the next day was a long-distance taxi ride to Kochi, a city on the coast. In deference to Helane's still-squeamish stomach, the driver cleared off the front passenger seat, his in-cab office, and she sat there. Dean, Piper and I settled in the back. Traveling with kids, Dean and I were traveling at a somewhat higher standard than we had without them. No more busses jammed with people, pigs and chickens.

In Kochi, a traditional spice trading capital, we stayed at a lovely old hotel. Bougainvillea covered the trellises and the open-air lobby was decorated with potted palms and oriental rugs. Our large family-sized room had black lattice shutters, a window seat and a slow-circling ceiling fan.

To get to the old port of Kochi, where bulk spices like nutmeg and ginger are still bought and sold, we took the ferry. It was made of wood and the blue paint was peeling. The captain sat in the second-story wheelhouse. The ferry catered to local traffic and we were the only tourists on board.

Disembarking from the ferry, we wandered along a street lined with spice houses. Men bartered over piles of ginger. The fragrance of cardamom filled the air. In one open cement courtyard, workers raked mounds of ginger roots into a single layer, then spread powdered lime on it to dry it out.

Through an open doorway, we saw seated women shaking whole nutmegs on wooden-framed wire screens. We ventured into the cool shade inside. A man was apparently in charge of the roomful of women workers. He seemed pleased by our interest and explained that the women were grading the nutmegs by size. Each woman had a different sized screen. A scoopful of nutmegs was tossed onto the largest screen. What did not fall through went into one bin—they were the largest and worth the most. The ones that fell through the screen into a basket were transferred to the woman with the next sized screen. The nutmegs that made it all the way through the series of declining screens were the least valuable. He offered to let the girls try shaking the screens. Shyly, they declined.

As we continued our exploration, the hot sun beat down on us. At the edge of the colonial-style spice buildings, we arrived at the oldest synagogue in India. A guide led us into the cool, dark interior. He explained the role of the Jews in the development of Kochi. I wondered how much of his explanation the girls understood. Then I realized it didn't matter: the atmosphere itself was powerful enough to make a lasting impression.

On the ferry back to our hotel, we realized we had more to explore and decided to return to the old town the next day.

In the morning, the ferry captain recognized us. He invited the girls to come up to the wheelhouse and help him pilot the ferry across. Helane declined, but Piper enthusiastically agreed. Dean helped her clamber up the roof over the passenger deck and the captain grabbed her hand and pulled her inside. She waved at us as we went below.

We spent the day meandering through old Kochi. We were beginning to understand the meaning of crossroads of civilizations, as we learned more about the history of this city. Native spices were first exported by Arab traders who came to the port. Then the Portuguese arrived, forcibly supplanting the Arabs. Then the Dutch beat out the Portuguese and the British fought and won against the Dutch. Finally, the British returned Kochi to its original owners. Each invader left its stamp on the city, layers of influence still visible. As we walked from one landmark to another, I couldn't help wondering how much the girls would remember of all this history.

On our way back to Trivandrum and our flight to Paris, we spent a day in Kuttenad, the Backwaters. There are no roads there, and the only way to see the area is by boat. As we stepped aboard the upper deck of the commercial boat, I felt very much the tourist. But as I looked at Dean and the girls, I realized that's exactly what we were, no mistaking it. And this service offered a way for us to see something otherwise inaccessible.

The boat slowly pulled away from the dock and we floated down the sluggish river which links the many canals in this water-centered world. This flat delta, sandwiched between the sea and the hills, is a completely rural region. Time slowed.

Everything and everyone moves on the calm water. Dense, dark vegetation alternates with dazzling green fields.

Villages line the canals' banks. Children splash in the shallows. Women wash clothes and spread them out to dry on the grass. Farmers plow the fields with buffalo. Flat-bottomed boats of varying description ply the waters.

At one point, we passed a stack of hay bales that appeared to be floating, there was so little of the boat visible underneath it. The boatman poled it away from the shore. But it was truly overloaded. The bow of the boat dipped. It did not reappear. The bales were sinking. The boatmen jumped off into chest-deep water. They steadied the boat, but there was nothing they could do. Their hopes sank into the brown waters.

During the course of the day, we unwound from our travels. Helane and Piper stretched out on the top deck. Tension floated upwards. Peacefulness penetrated our skin along with the sun's rays. At the end of the day, reluctantly, we headed for Trivandrum and our journey home.

Our visit to India did not repel the girls, as I had once feared. We offered them experiences, and Helane and Piper took something from them. Before we left Trivandrum, Helane had already given it some thought. She declared: "I want to walk across India some day."

Winegeese

~

They flew from Ireland with a specific purpose in mind. Unlike the hundreds of thousands of who fled Ireland in successive waves following the Great Famine and political disruptions, seeking a better life wherever opportunity could be found, the Winegeese knew where they were going. They sought opportunities in the lucrative wine trade and headed to the source of great French wine: Bordeaux.

Probably introduced by the Phoenicians, wine has been appreciated and highly valued in Ireland for over two thousand years. Perhaps because grape vines could not be successfully cultivated in Erin's overcast climate, wine achieved a particular status as a rare commodity.

In the time of the Phoenicians, wine production had spread from its origin in the Caucasus region to the Mediterranean basin. The Greeks, in particular, developed various strains of wine grapes. Together, the Greeks and Phoenicians spread these vines all the way to the Atlantic coast.

Indefatigable traders, the Phoenicians opened a route from the Mediterranean across today's France, through the Carcassonne Gap, down the Garonne River to the Bay of Biscay. From there, they traveled north along the coast, reaching Ireland and Cornwall from the Celtic Sea. The

Phoenicians brought amphora of wine. They took back Irish implements and ornaments and valuable Cornish tin.

Feasting at the great courts of ancient Ireland was renowned. During the fifth through seventh centuries, the central seat of authority was at Tara, where the High Kings resided. In the poem "Tara of the Kings," from *The Grey Feet of the Wind*, Cathal O'Byrne describes such a feast,

> *The tables groaned beneath the mighty weight*
> *Of ponderous vats of rare and precious wines,*
> *And carcases of oxen roasted whole,*
> *Methers of foaming mead went gaily round*
> *From lip to lip, and friend and foe alike*
> *Ate, drank, and quaffed their brimming cups,*
> *Forgetting for the moment every wrong*
> *That ever held them sundered. Such the Law.*

Centuries later, wine was used as a medium of taxation. In the ninth century, the Vikings developed the port towns of southern Ireland: Cork, Waterford, Limerick, Wexford and Dublin. According to Ted Murphy, in his book *The Kingdom of Wine*, in the eleventh century, "the tribute system existed in Ireland and the Vikings of Limerick paid an annual tribute to King Brian Boru at his palace in Kincora on the Shannon, which consisted of a ton of wine for every day in the year." Translated into modern day seventy-five centiliter bottles of wine, that is one thousand five hundred and thirty-six bottles of wine for every day in the year. No wonder wine flowed freely in the king's banquet halls.

The connection between Ireland and Bordeaux drew closer in the twelfth century. In 1159, King Henry II received the title "Lord of Ireland" from Pope Adrian IV and, with it the Pope's blessing to invade the island. His Anglo-Norman army invaded Ireland and ultimately established control over much of the country. King Henry II's many territories included his wife Eleanor of Aquitaine's dowry, Bordeaux and many of the other wine-growing regions of France. Geraldus Cambrensis, a member of King Henry II's entourage, wrote in *The Topography of Ireland* in 1177, "Imported wines, however, conveyed in the ordinary commercial way, are so abundant that you would scarcely notice that the vine was neither cultivated nor gave its fruit there. Poitou out of its own superabundance sends plenty of wine, and Ireland is pleased to send in return the hides and animal skins of flocks and wild beasts."

The new Anglo-Norman establishment added its demand for wine to that of the traditional Gaelic chieftains. Wine trade with France flourished and Ireland itself became a center of wine trade. In 1412, the Vintage Fleet comprised some one hundred and sixty vessels plying to and fro from Bordeaux. It included five Irish ships, three from Kinsale and two from Dublin.

Wine was enjoyed at all levels of society. It was not limited to the upper classes. In 1735, George Berkeley in *The Querist* wrote that "while in England many gentlemen with one thousand pounds a year never drank wine in their houses, in Ireland this could hardly be said of any who had one hundred pounds a year."

But flourishing trade itself attracts taxation. By the sixteenth century, heavy duties were imposed by the English on the importation of wine into Ireland. The independent Irish countered by developing their own "free trade" in wine—

known to the English Crown as smuggling. In an effort to stem free trade, the British government enacted legislation that recognized only certain cities where wine could legally enter the country. Among these were Cork City and Kinsale. In Kinsale, Desmond Castle became the Customs House and through it passed great quantities of imported wine. Today Desmond Castle houses the International Museum of Wine. Cork City wine families of note included Roache, Morrogh, Gallwey, Lawton and McCarthy. Descendents of these families were among the first Winegeese—Irish who emigrated to France to trade in wine.

Even for the merchants who profited from their privileged position in an approved port city, the restrictive legislation was burdensome. Added to the tumultuous political situation in Ireland in the seventeenth and eighteenth centuries, it inspired up-and-coming youth to seek their fortunes elsewhere. Bordeaux, the source of some of the best French wines imported in Ireland, was an attractive destination.

Abraham Lawton of County Cork was one of the most successful Winegeese. Establishing the wine brokerage house of Tastet and Lawton in Bordeaux in 1739, he became an outstanding leader in the wine trade. He has been described as "one of the most influential figures in the wine history of Bordeaux," and "all powerful."

As foreigners, the Winegeese were prohibited from carrying out their trade within the city limits of Bordeaux. So they built their warehouses and homes along the Quai des Chartrons. Due to the wealth they created, the Chartronnais district became more beautiful than the city center. Irish traders shipped wine to Ireland and Ireland shipped back salted beef and butter. Eventually, Winegeese married into local wine-producing families and purchased vineyards of their own. They became part of some of the most renowned names in Bordeaux wines: Chateau Lynch-Bages, Chateau Latour, Chateau Leoville-Barton, Chateau Phelan-Segur, Chateau Siran, Chateau MacCarthy (now part of Chateau Haut-Marbuzet), Chateau Giscours and Chateau d'Yquem (McMahon family). Some Winegeese families, for example the Johnstons, maintain their presence on the Quai de Chartrons to this day: Nathaniel Johnston of Armagh founded Nathanial Johnston et Fils, now run by brothers Denis, Archibald and Ivanhoe Johnston.

Other seventeenth and eighteenth century Winegeese of note include Thomas Barton of County Fermanagh, Peter Mitchell of Dublin, Patrice MacMahon of Limerick, James Lynch of Galway, Bernard Phelan of Clonmel, and Denis McCarthy of Cork.

In 1787, Thomas Jefferson followed the ancient Phoenician trade route from the Mediterranean to the Garonne River and thus to the Bay of Biscay and the Atlantic. Unlike the ancient route, however, Jefferson made the voyage on a barge towed along the *Canal des Deux Mers*, also known as the *Canal du Midi*. Pierre Paul Riquet masterminded the building of the canal and the reservoirs that maintain its water supply. The Canal was completed in 1681, shortly following Riquet's death, and added considerably to the prosperity of Bordeaux, located where the Garonne River enters the Atlantic. During his trip along the Canal, Jefferson sampled local wines and kept notes in his journal on his favorites. When he arrived in Bordeaux, Jefferson was advised by a member of the Lawton family regarding wines to purchase for his *cave* in Paris. Following his return to the

United States, Jefferson introduced George Washington to the wine of Bordeaux and purchased cases of wine for both of them, to be delivered by ship from Bordeaux to America.

The Johnston family developed the American connection, sending a representative to the United States in 1807. The trip was a commercial success and Winegeese Nathanial Johnston and Fils entered the New World. Ireland maintained its position as an entrepôt of wines: many of the wines shipped from Bordeaux passed through Ireland on their way to America.

Other Winegeese entered the New World as growers and traders. Dominic Lynch, with Galway roots, became a wine merchant in New York in 1785. He imported chateau-bottled wines from France and Madiera wine from that island.

Bernard MacMahon was born in Ireland in 1775. At twenty-one, he emigrated to the United States and established a horticultural center near Philadelphia. Although wine grapes were not being grown commercially in the United States at that time, MacMahon conducted pioneering experiments grafting vines. He also advocated hybridization as a way to develop vines suitable for the American climate. His advice proved correct and hybridization and grafting are standard practices throughout the world today.

James Concannon, born in the Aran Islands, purchased property in Livermore Valley, California in 1883, and planted a vineyard intending to make wine for the Catholic Church. He traveled to France and purchased root stock from the McMahon's Chateau d'Yquem, which he brought back and planted in Livermore. In 1889, Concannon traveled to Mexico and obtained a concession from the Mexican government to sell grape stock to local vintners. In five years, Concannon shipped millions of cuttings to Mexican growers, greatly impacting Mexican viticulture.

Wineries in California with Winegeese connections include Christopher Buckley's Ravenswood; Dan Gainey's Gainey Winery; Bob Travers Mayacamas Vineyards; Jack Cakebread's Cakebread Cellars; Robert Foley of Robert Foley Vineyards; Michael Collins of Limerick Lane Cellars; Jim Barrett's Chateau Montelena; Molly Chappellet of Chappellet Winery; Francis Mahoney of Carneros Creek Winery; and Mike Lee of Kenwood Vineyards.

Winegeese also traveled Down Under. Samuel McWilliam of Northern Ireland emigrated to Australia in 1857. With the planting of his first vineyard in 1877, he established McWilliams Wines, still producing wine today. The region he opened to viticulture is known as the Riverina, which accounts for two-thirds of wine production in New South Wales and nearly one-quarter in all of Australia.

The Cullen family, descended from a Wexford County Clarke who arrived in Australia in the eighteenth century, opened the Margaret River as a wine-producing region.

The Murphy family arrived in Australia from Cork in the 1860's. They established Trentham Estates in New South Wales in 1909. Murphy family members continue to run the business.

Other Winegeese flew as far as New Zealand, South Africa and Chile, developing vineyards and the wine trading businesses as they settled in their new homes.

But the story does not end with emigration. Ireland, which historically was not a wine-producing country, has become one. In 2000, the European Commission listed Ireland as a wine producer. The change has been brought about by work related to that of Brian MacMahon, one of the Winegeese who, in 1796, emigrated to the United States. The work MacMahon pioneered in the hybridization of grape varieties has continued. In 1964 in Czechoslavkia, Professor V. Kraus successfully crossed the varieties Zarya Severa and St. Larent to produce the Rondo grape. According to Irish wine writer Tomas Clancy, the Rondo grape "matures early and is resistant to frost and the harsh Irish climactic conditions. It ripens well in Irish summers and produces a pretty deep ruby red wine with a velvety, almost merlot-wash."

The Rondo grape is now being grown successfully in Ireland by David Llewellyn at his Lusk vineyard outside Dublin. In addition to his Rondo red wine, Llewellyn produces a popular sauvignon blanc. In the south, in Counties Waterford and Cork, credible wines are also being produced. Blackwater Valley Vineyard produces several thousand bottles of Reichensteiner white wine yearly. Longueville House Hotel produces just enough Reichensteiner and Muller Thurgau white wine to serve at its restaurant. Thomas Walk Vineyard near Kinsale grows the Amurensis grape, known for its durability in cold weather and named for the Amur River in northern China. The red wine has been described as a "light Beaujolais." The Irish vineyards are nascent, and promising.

As I sit with my friend on a terrace overlooking the harbor in Kinsale, we raise our wine glasses, filled with ruby red Bordeaux, to the Winegeese. They left Ireland to engage in the business of buying, selling and creating wine. With vineyards now prospering in Eire, they may be able to begin the long migration home.

Pangur Bán

~

Wending my way through the exhibition at the Book of Kells, I stopped short at the ceiling-high panel of a poem.

> *I and Pangur Bán, my cat*
> *'Tis a like task we are at;*
> *Hunting mice is his delight*
> *Hunting words I sit all night.*
>
> *Better far than praise of men*
> *'Tis to sit with book and pen;*
> *Pangur bears me no ill will,*
> *He too plies his simple skill.*
>
> *'Tis a merry thing to see*
> *At our tasks how glad are we,*
> *When at home we sit and find*
> *Entertainment to our mind.*
>
> *Oftentimes a mouse will stray*
> *In the hero Pangur's way:*
> *Oftentimes my keen thought set*
> *Takes a meaning in its net.*

*'Gainst the wall he sets his eye
Full and fierce and sharp and sly;
'Gainst the wall of knowledge I
All my little wisdom try.*

*When a mouse darts from its den,
O how glad is Pangur then!
O what gladness do I prove
When I solve the doubts I love!*

*So in peace our tasks we ply,
Pangur Bán, my cat, and I;
In our arts we find our bliss,
I have mine and he has his.*

*Practice every day has made
Pangur perfect in his trade;
I get wisdom day and night
Turning darkness into light.*

Unable to memorize it on the spot, I bought a copy at the bookstore on the way out. Many have translated this poem from Gaelic and it has been alternately attributed to a student, a scholar, or a monk. Seamus Heaney's translation entitled "Pangur Bán" begins,

*Pangur Bán and I at work,
Adepts, equals, cat and clerk:
His whole instinct is to hunt,
fine to free the meaning pent.*

Frank O'Connor's translation entitled "The Scholar and the Cat" begins,

> *Each of us pursues his trade,*
> *I and Pangur my comrade,*
> *His whole fancy on the hunt,*
> *And mine for learning ardent.*

The full translation above—the one I love—is by Robin Flower, entitled "The Student and His Cat." The anonymous author of the poem immortalized his work on the margins of a copy of the Epistles in the ninth century. He was working at St. Paul's Monastery on Reichenau Island in Lake Constance (Bodensee), where Germany borders Carinthia, Austria. I was surprised to learn that this favorite Irish poem was actually written in Austria. But as I began to learn about the history of Irish-founded monasteries, it wasn't surprising at all.

Irish monasteries had developed into great centers of scholarship in the 500s C.E. By the 600s, there were dozens of monasteries, some as large as Clonard, Bangor and Clonfert with 3,000 or more monks each. Others comprised hundreds of monks. In contrast to other branches of the Catholic Church, the Irish Church was "in the world," serving its congregants. St. Augustine and St. Martin of Tours had expressed a similar concept: monks were the servants, not the masters, of their flock.

Irish monasteries were based on the principle of self-support: they raised their own food and did not rely on gifts or taxes from the local population. In addition to copying manuscripts for distribution, they provided free education to local children as well as those of the affluent aristocracy. Children were schooled from age seven to seventeen: the first son and the first daughter in a family were accepted. Some—but not all—of the children of a family might receive an education. Most students were expected to return to secular life after completing their education. They became bilingual in Latin and studied Greek; poems, stories and laws were taught in Gaelic. Foreigners traveled from abroad to study in Ireland.

The monastic centers of learning produced advances in mechanical engineering, botany, zoology and agronomy. The latter included such apparently mundane advances as plows with metal collars, as well as sophisticated methods of harnessing water power, which allowed the expansion of arable land. The monasteries became the centers of agricultural communities. Population around the monasteries increased as they attracted craftsmen and artisans, metalworkers and carvers, painters and goldsmiths. Each monastery included a scriptorium for the copying of manuscripts.

But the unfortified monasteries were subject to attack from the sea, first from Irish clan barons, then from the Vikings, who looted, burned manuscripts and sometimes murdered the monks. In the late sixth century, the emigration of Irish monks began. In 565, Columba traveled to Scotland to establish monasteries. Fifteen years later, his friend, compatriot and fellow poet Columban traveled with twelve disciples to establish monasteries in France and the rest of Europe. In addition to founding monasteries, both Columba and Columban made significant innovations in poetry.

Before his death in 615, Columban and his immediate followers, eventually amounting to several thousand

~ India, Ireland and Italy ~

monks from Ireland, established forty monasteries on the Continent. They used the same teaching methods they had developed at home. From the standpoint of education, the period from 500-800 has been described as a "mass-literacy movement." As they had in Ireland, the monks taught Latin and Greek and also created dictionaries, compiling words and expressions so they could teach in local vernacular languages, French, German, and Italian. Between 575 and 725, the Irish monastic movement founded one hundred and thirteen monasteries and schools in France and Switzerland, twenty-six in Germany, ten in Austria and three in the north of Italy.

The monasteries were schools and the schools were scriptoria, from which new copies of the Scriptures and other religious writings were dispersed throughout Europe. The student, scholar, or monk who wrote Pangur Bán found himself in just such a scriptorium in the 800s.

He was not the only copyist to write in the margins of the manuscript upon which he was working. Kuno Meyer translated "The Blackbird," written by a monk in the margin of a book he was copying in the seventh century:

> *Ah, blackbird, thou art satisfied*
> *Where thy nest is in the bush:*
> *Hermit that clinkest no bell,*
> *Sweet, soft, peaceful is thy note.*

Of religious significance, a nine-verse poem was found in the margin of a ninth century Latin Juvencus manuscript. Six of the nine verses are explicitly trinitarian, that is, containing a reference to the Holy Trinity. This is the earliest example of the trinitarian poetic tradition written in Welsh. The books being copied were important, but the poems in the margins are also an important legacy.

Just one day after visiting the Book of Kells exhibition at Trinity College in Dublin, a friend and I found ourselves in Kinsale, taking refuge from the rain in the Armada Pub. Two musicians held forth, an Irish folk singer playing the guitar and a drummer. We joined the enthusiastic crowd, clapping and singing along whenever we could. Later, the singer joined us. We complimented him on his repertoire.

He graciously thanked us, then informed us that folk singing was not his greatest interest. His greatest interest was bringing Celtic culture into the lives of Irish youth. He takes ancient Celtic rhymes and turns them into modern music: rap. He pulled a set of keys out of his pocket, closed them lightly in his fingers and, shaking the keys, established the beat. He began rapping,

> *I and Pangur Bán my cat,*
> *Tis a like task we are at:*
> *Hunting nice is his delight,*
> *Hunting words I sit all night...*

Mussel Farming in Taranto

~

At the Hotel Ristorante Orsa Maggiore near Santa Cesarea, I sampled *Cozze d'Otranto*; at L'Ancora Ristorante near Monopoli, the mussels were served *all'Ancora* over tagliolini in a rich sauce with clams and shrimp; at Don Carmelo's Ristorante Pizzeria in Alberobello, the mussels were served in a casserole. It seemed every restaurant in Puglia had its own favorite—and delectable—way of preparing mussels.

I have eaten mussels elsewhere in Europe. In Brussels, Belgium I have eaten mounds of steamed mussels in a delicately flavored broth served with crisp French fries. On Ile de Re in France, I have eaten them in a creamy curry sauce. In Neapolis, Greece, I have eaten them on the half shell, baked, smothered in Saganaki cheese and tomatoes.

But the plumpest, juiciest, most succulent mussels I have ever tasted were in Puglia. As a mussel aficionado, I had to learn more about these exceptional examples of my favorite shellfish, *Mytilus galloprovincialis*.

It was no great surprise to learn that the largest mussel farm in Italy is in Taranto, producing about twelve thousand tons of mussels per year. According to one source, "The Mar Piccolo of Taranto represents a pattern of enclosed coastal marine ecosystem in which the intense activity of mussel culture makes it the most important mussel farming [location] in Italy."

Taranto is a port city located on the Ionian Sea on the western coast of Puglia. On the inner edge of the Mar Grande of Taranto, there is a narrow opening leading to the Mar Piccolo, a lagoon that is itself divided into two basins, the Primo Seno and the Secundo Seno. A total of thirty-four freshwater springs, as well as several small rivers, feed into Mar Piccolo, diluting the sea water that enters from the Mar Grande. Mussels thrive in this semi-saline solution.

Taranto, known as Taras by its original Greek settlers, then as Tarentum by it Roman rulers, has been renowned for mussel production for twenty-five centuries. Pliny and Virgil referred to the mussels of Taras in their writings. Documents dating from 1204 to 1395 indicate that the Roman Catholic Church, recognizing the commercial importance of mussels, had laid claim to certain fishing rights. By the fifteenth century, the industry was important enough to be regulated by fishing laws inscribed in the *Libro Russo*, the *Directorium Dohanaarum Rubrum*, of the Taranto princes.

The earliest Greek settlers picked mussels up out of the mud in the shallow waters of the Mar Piccolo. They discovered how to use tree branches to create rakes with long tines, which they used to rake mussels together into mounds. They shoveled the mounds of mussels into baskets to carry home or to sell.

Although mussels may grow unattached in the sea bed, they prefer to attach themselves to something—a rock, stick or piece of rope. In the sixteenth century, Giovine described mussel tilling techniques. In the seventeenth century, Giannattasio described a special technique used to farm mussels that involved half-burying *bouchòts* (pine stakes) in the sea bed. According to Giannatttasio, a crusader who had stopped in Taranto on his return from the Middle East learned the technique and passed it on to mussel fisherman throughout Europe.

In the sixteenth and seventeenth centuries, mussel production reached a new level. Fishermen established their first cooperatives in an attempt to free themselves from the commercial control of the Roman Catholic Church and local lords. Data from a land registry of 1746 shows a total of 493 fishermen and 19 tenants of mussel fishing grounds.

In the second half of the eighteenth century, mussel farmers discovered that mussels would firmly attach themselves to the fibers of a lightly woven rope. They developed a system that employed *zoche* (cane ropes) specially spun by a rope maker using an iron wheel called in local dialect *la rota ti lu fiskalaru*. Mussel farmers tied the *zoche* to stakes which were anchored in the fishing ground, the stake tops reaching upwards through the water's surface like outstretched arms. Farmers hung mussels in the ropes, weaving them in pairs into the *zoche*. The young mussels grew suspended in their *zoche* from October to April, when they were fully grown and could be harvested and sold.

During the reign of King Ferdinando II di Borbone from 1810-1859, productive water properties were divided up between feudal lords and religious orders.

In 1900, Augustus J.C. Hare wrote in his book *Cities of Southern Italy and Sicily*, "The principal curiosity of Taranto is the Mar Piccolo (about six miles long and three miles broad), with its active industries of fisheries and the propagation of fish....The mode of farming mussels is that which was in existence in the twelfth century. Ropes are plunged into the water, and, when festooned with shells, are drawn up, and carried to the market, where the purchaser chooses his mussels himself, makes his bargain, and then has them detached."

The Mar Piccolo continued as a fishing preserve—for numerous species of fish as well as mussels and oysters—until 1889. In that year, the Italian government decided to locate the Royal Arsenal in Mar Piccolo, thus changing the character of its natural habitat.

Today, aquaculture and commercial fishing in Mar Piccolo are subject to the combined pressures of urbanization, industrialization and agriculture. From the surrounding urban communities including Taranto, fourteen pipes discharge sewage into Mar Piccolo. The shipyard of the Italian Navy, including its dry docks, is located in the Primo Seno. Chemicals used by farmers in their fields outside Taranto leach into the water table or are carried as runoff into the rivers that feed into the Mar Piccolo.

Mussels are very sensitive to the water that surrounds them. Filter feeders, they quickly register any contaminants in their environment in their own flesh. For that reason, they are considered bio-indicators. Since the early 1900s, they have been the focus of many studies in the Mar Piccolo. Scientists can tell the health of the ecosystem by studying the health of the mussels living there.

The largest concentration of mussel farms in Italy using the "fixed" culturing system is located in the Gulf of Taranto, Puglia. Other traditional mussel-producing coastal and lagoon regions include La Spezia in Liguria, the Venetian Lagoon and the Flegreen Coast in Campania. More recent additions include the Friuli-Venezia Guilia coastal area of Trieste, the Gulf of Olbia in Sardegna, Emilia-Romagna and the Adriatic coast of Puglia. In addition to the "fixed" culturing system, *monoventia* (single long line) and Trieste *multiventia* (multiple long lines) systems are used.

The most recent development in mussel farming has been off-shore technologies that allow mussels to be grown outside lagoons and coastal areas—avoiding many environmental, health and hygiene problems. Off-shore mussels are grown using a suspension culture technique, evolved from the lagoon technique, that involves a floating structure, either on the surface or submerged, from which ropes are suspended. Off-shore production is carried out in Taranto, Mattinata, the Gulf of Trieste and the Gulf of Manfredonia.

The extensive commercial production of mussels has made them easily available. Easy availability has led creative cooks to devise many ways to serve them. Versatile, mussels can be steamed, fried, baked, or grilled, served plain or in a sauce. Every way, they are delicious.

In Puglia's provinces of Brindisi, Lecce and Taranto, a familiar dish is *Cozze alla Maniera Salentina*. Here is one way to prepare it:

Ingredients

12 ounces or 300 grams of live mussels (these must be allowed to purge by soaking them for 24 hours in heavily salted water in the refrigerator)

1 pound or 500 grams of peeled, sliced potatoes

1 sliced white onion

1 small bunch minced parsley

2 tablespoons breadcrumbs

2 tablespoons grated pecorino cheese

2 beaten eggs

Olive oil

Sea salt and freshly ground pepper to taste

Directions

Scrub the mussels and pry them open over a bowl, saving the water from the shells. Put the mussels in a separate bowl and discard the shells.

In a pan that can be used in the oven, cook the sliced potatoes, onion and half the parsley in the water from the mussels and a little olive oil. Remove all but a thin layer of potato slices and place a thin layer of mussels on top of it. Dust the mussel layer with breadcrumbs, cheese and minced parsley.

Follow with a second layer of potatoes, mussels, breadcrumbs, cheese and parsley. Pour the beaten egg over the top.

Bake in a hot oven at 440* F. or 220* C. until the upper surface is crisp and golden.

If there is not enough time to prepare the dish above, *Spaghetti alle Cozze* is a tasty alternative:

Scrub the mussels and pry them open over a bowl, saving the water from the shells. Put the mussels in a separate bowl.

~ India, Ireland and Italy ~

Heat olive oil with garlic slivers in a large pan, add fresh ground pepper and the mussels with a little of their own water. Add drained spaghetti, cooked very al dente, to the pan with the mussels. Add the rest of the mussel water and some of the water used to cook the pasta, if necessary. Sprinkle with chopped parsley and more fresh ground pepper.

Magna Graecia

~

"Acquire land and found a city where you see rain falling from a clear sky," the Oracle at Delphi had pronounced. What kind of instructions were those? How could Phalanthos lead a group of colonists all the way across the sea to that far peninsula with only that to go on?

Other aspiring Greek colonists had been given better directions. Following the famine twenty-six years before, the Chalcidians, for example, had received instructions to found their city at the mouth of the Apia River. That was a place one could look for. And by all accounts, Rhegion was now a flourishing city in Calabria.

Besides, Phalanthos had heard that Sikonyia was a desirable location. He could happily take his followers there. He would go back and ask for a blessing to settle somewhere he had at least heard of. Accompanied by Partheniai, his best friend from Sparta, Phalanthos returned to the Oracle.

The Oracle replied, "Fair is the land between Corinth and Sikyon, but you will not settle there. Look to Satyrion, the water of Taras, a harbor to the left, and the place where the goat loves salt water, wetting the tip of his grey beard. There build Taras."

The Oracle rarely gave the answer one wanted to one's questions. All right then, he would not go to Sikonyia, he would follow the edge of the narrow peninsula until he passed Satyrion and would find the next best harbor. Satyrion had been established about the same time as Rhegion. As far as he had heard, the local inhabitants had tolerated the new settlers. But Phalanthos would take no unnecessary chances. He would find a location that could be defended from attack.

The winds had been fair all the way from Arcadia. The voyagers had been at sea for four days, out of sight of land for the last two.

The coast of Puglia appeared first as a vague blue line on the horizon, barely distinguishable from the sea. As the voyagers watched, hour after hour, the line grew firm, details appeared. The coast varied from imposing stone cliffs, to hills, to flat terrain. But Phalanthos sailed on, searching for the ideal landing. Following the coastline as it turned north, he continued on until they came to a large bay. At the inner edge of the bay he found a narrow entrance into a small secluded harbor. There he dropped anchor. On this spit of land he would found the city the Oracle had named Taras.

The year was 706 BCE. The voyagers were Spartans, sent as colonists from their mother-city, their *metropolis*. The colonists were seeking a land of opportunity; Sparta was seeking a connection for commerce and trade. The colonists had brought with them some of the sacred fire from the public hearth in Sparta. They would use it to kindle the public hearth of their new settlement. Taras would maintain its connection to its mother city for centuries, regularly sending gifts and representatives back to Sparta. When Taras grew strong enough to send out its own colonists, it consulted Sparta in advance.

The colonists found a hospitable countryside, land that was stony but fertile, surrounded by the bounteous sea. They cleared the stones from the fields, using them to build stone fences that stretched for miles. They planted roots of olive trees and grapevines they had carried with them from home. They buried their dead in a necropolis outside the city walls. As Taras grew, they built piazzas and temples in the style of Arcadia. Two Doric columns of the Temple of Poseidon still grace the waterfront of Taras, Rome's Tarentum, today's Taranto.

Meanwhile, other Greek city-states were sending out their own colonists to establish outposts on the shores of the Italian peninsula. More than thirty city-states established multiple colonies, spread from the southern coast of the Iberian peninsula (today's Spain) to the shores of the Black Sea (today's Turkey). Important Greek colonies in today's Italy were Rhegion, established by Chalcis; Syracuse, by Corinth; Cyme, by Aeolis; Ischia and Cuma (near Naples) by Chalcis; and Elea (Velia) in Campania by Phocaea. Other Greek colonies included Naples, Akragas, Subaris, Locri, Cortone, Turii, Gallipoli and Ancona. Magna Graecia, as the region was called, spread from Sicily through the south of the boot-shaped peninsula, from Calabria on the tip of the boot, to Puglia, its high heel.

The Greeks established permanent colonies and actively traded throughout the region. Archeologists trace the trading activities of these ancient Greeks by the troves of Greek coins they have uncovered.

The Greeks also brought their alphabet with them. The Chalcidean/Cumaean form of the Greek alphabet was first adopted by the Etruscans, who had arrived in the north of the peninsula about a hundred years before the Greeks arrived in the south. The Etruscan alphabet evolved into the Latin alphabet, the most widely-used alphabet in the world.

Greek colonists in Puglia lived in uneasy proximity with the Messapii, people who had arrived from Illyria (today's Albania) several hundred years before the first Greeks arrived. The Messapii lived in heavily fortified cities including Manduria and Oria. Though they competed for control of the countryside, the Greeks dominated the Puglian coast, from today's Bari to Otranto to Taranto. At Egnazia, the Greeks overran the Messapii and turned the city into a model sea port. Today, the ruins are a protected archeological site, with a museum of treasures recovered from the graves of both Messapii and Greeks.

Although marred by periodic wars against each other, both cultures flourished side-by-side until the Roman armies descended on the south. The Greeks and Messapii united under King Pyrrhus of Epirus to fight against the enemy from the north. From 280 to 275 BCE, battles raged. But even their combined strength was not enough. Following the Pyrrhic War, both Magna Graecia and Messapia were absorbed into the Roman Empire.

Latin replaced Greek as the language of the learned, sophisticated ruling class. However, the Greek language survived among its subjugated speakers as the language of laborers, used within families at home.

For almost six hundred years, Roman rule was absolute in former Magna Graecia. When Theodosius I died in 395

CE, the Roman Empire was divided between his two sons. The Western Roman Empire was overrun by the Goths in the fourth century, and by the fifth century had disintegrated into a patchwork of warring kingdoms. The Eastern Roman Empire, with its capital in Constantinople, remained intact and strong. Greek replaced Latin as the official language of the Empire, and the Eastern Roman Empire became known as the Byzantine Empire. Emperor Justinian I, who ruled from 527-565 CE, reestablished the Empire's control over the south of Italy. His Greek- speaking troops found a sympathetic population of Greek speakers in the former Magna Graecia. Waves of Orthodox Christian Greeks arrived from Greece and the eastern Mediterranean during the Early Middle Ages. They established Greek Orthodox churches and monasteries throughout Puglia. The most important of these monasteries was St. Nicola di Casole in the Salentine region, a monastery, cultural center and school, with a particularly rich library. Manuscripts from the library are now housed in museums including those in Florence, the Vatican City, Paris, London and Berlin.

However, this renaissance of Magna Graecia was once again threatened from the north, first by the Lombards, then by the Normans. Pope Nicolo II wanted to establish Roman Catholic rule over the south and, with the Melfi Agreement of 1059 CE, legitimized the Norman campaign. Although the Normans established the Roman Catholic Church in Puglia, the Greek Orthodox Church survived in certain areas, such as the Salento, for another five hundred years. During the Counter-Reformation in the sixteenth century, Rome officially abolished Greek Orthodox rites.

~ *India, Ireland and Italy* ~

When the Normans drove out the Byzantine administration, Latin once again replaced Greek as the official language of the region. But the Greek language survived in small pockets, including certain towns around Lecce, in Salento province.

Today, there are two areas of the former Magna Graecia where Greek is still spoken: in Reggio Calabria, the very tip of the toe of Italy's boot, and in Grecia Salentina in Puglia. Although the dialects have evolved over the centuries, speakers of Grecanico in Calabria can converse with speakers of Griko in Salento. Linguists debate whether today's Griko and Grecanico derive from the original Greek colonists or from the Byzantine Middle Ages. Because many ancient Greek words are found in both dialects, the consensus is that the Greek dialects spoken today descend from the first colonists in the 700s BCE.

The government of Italy has recognized both communities as official linguistic minorities and the European Union has granted Griko status as an endangered language. The result of this official recognition has given Griko-speaking communities the right to use the language in street signs and in radio broadcasts and to teach Griko language and culture in elementary schools.

As the Greek language survived the centuries, so did other aspects of Greek culture, including Greek music. When the Greek Orthodox church was banned, believers sang their Mass in Greek in the streets. Today, during Holy Week, *I Passiuna tu Christù* (Christ's Passion) is performed by two street singers accompanied by an accordion player. Similarly, *La Strina* is a song about the birth and infancy of Christ.

The *taranta*, a popular folk dance of Puglia, was traditionally danced by women who would twirl ecstatically until they collapsed, exhausted. The *taranta* is reputedly descended from the rituals of the cult of Dionysus, the ancient Greek god of wine, in which his followers, the Bacchae, would dance ecstatically until collapse.

The grapevines brought by Greek colonists to Puglia, the genesis of wine itself, have also survived the centuries. Several varietals, now considered native to Puglia, were actually introduced to the peninsula from Greece. According to legend, Aeneas, leading the few survivors of Troy to settle in Italy, carried the *Uva di Troia* (Grapes of Troy) with him. *Negro Amaro* grapes, thriving around the Bay of Taranto, may have been brought to Puglia by Pharanthos himself. *Negro Amaro* grapes are often blended with *Malvasia Nera di Lecce*, *Malvasia* being another variety of grapes that originated in Greece around Monemvasia. *Aglianico, Grecanico* and *Greco* varietals were also introduced to Italy by some of the original Greek colonists. For the early colonists, selling wine to Greek colonies in Africa was a lucrative trade. Wine made from these grapes is still lucrative trade in Puglia.

On a recent trip to Puglia, I sat with a friend in a small piazza, drinking a glass of wine from the DOC (Certified Original Location) of Salice Salentino Rosso. The ruby red wine was a *Leverano Vigna Del Saraceno Malvasia*, bottled by the Conti Zecca Estate. We were in the town of Calimera, whose name means "good morning" in Greek. Its whitewashed buildings, baking in the strong sun, looked like any other small town in Puglia, except for its street signs. They were written in Greek—names in Italian appearing on the second line. At a nearby table, two old men conversed in a language that sounded like Greek. The excellent wine was from vines of Greek origin; the language surrounding us was Greek; we were reading signs written in the Greek alphabet. Yes, we were in Puglia. But we were in one of the nine towns of Puglia called the Grecia Salentina, where the heritage of Magna Graecia remains clear.

On an ancient Greek burial stone in a small park in Calimera is the inscription: *Zeni su en ise ettù sti Kalimera* (You are not a stranger here in Calimera). If Phalanthos were here today, he would feel at home.

~

CHAPTER FIVE

~

Greece

Vines of Vatika

~

The Greek god Dionysus gave the gift of wine to man. He showed mortals how to cultivate vineyards, then he taught them the art of turning grapes into wine. Dionysus is a god of transformation: transforming grapes into wine and ordinary humans into beings filled with god, that is en-*theos*-asm, enthusiasm," Thanasis Maskaleris explained. An expert on Dionysus and Apollo, he shared his insights with us on the hillside in Mesochori. As he spoke, I looked at the tapestry of vineyards and olive groves on the slopes rolling down to the bright blue sea.

The Greeks learned Dionysus' lessons early on and learned them well. Indigenous varieties of grapes were cultivated and harvested and turned into a dark, sweet wine. In ancient times, enterprising Greek colonists and the ubiquitous Phoenician traders spread the art of cultivating vineyards and producing wine to the west as far as the Atlantic coast.

By the 1100's, large quantities of wines were being exported from the Peloponnese. The sweet wine made in Vatika near the island fortress of Monemvasia has been called "one of the most visible and enduring medieval Greek wines."

As it was exported, its name evolved and it became known throughout Europe as malvasia or malmsey.

When the Byzantine Empire fell to the Crusaders in 1204, the European Crusaders gained access to Greek vineyards. In a second wave of exportation, Crusaders took local vines home with them, transplanting them throughout the Mediterranean basin, in Italy, France, Spain and Portugal.

By the mid-1400's, malmsey had become a popular wine in England and reputedly the favorite libation of the Royal Duke of Clarence. In Shakespeare's *Richard II*, when the First Murderer stabs Clarence, he says: "Take that, and that: if all this will not do, I'll drown you in the malmsey-butt within." And rumor has it Clarence drowned.

When Spanish explorers reached the New World, they carried with them grape vines from the Mediterranean basin—some of them varieties that had originated in Greece. By the mid-1500's, Greek grape vines were growing in Mexico, Brazil, Argentina, Panama, Peru and Chile.

Back to the Roots

Grape vines still thrive in the climate of Vatika. In Greece, there are basically two types of climates in which vines thrive: inland climates such as in the highlands near Tripoli and island climates where the sea winds cool the sun-warmed hillsides. From a grapevine's point of view, Vatika, with its long shoreline, is an island climate.

In the Biblical book of Isaiah it says, "And every man beneath his vine and fig tree shall live in peace and unafraid." The grapevine and the fig tree are symbols of security and

~ Greece ~

the good life that may be enjoyed in times of peace. In Vatika, grapevines and fig trees have traditionally surrounded every whitewashed house. Making wine following the grape harvest in September was a family tradition. There is a self-sufficiency in Vatika that, coming from the United States, I always associated with pioneers. Now I realize the pioneers were only carrying on the traditional ways they had learned from their own ancestors. In Vatika, that meant growing one's own grapevines for wine, one's own olive trees to produce olives for the table and for olive oil, one's own lemons for flavoring all foods, and fig trees for figs to be eaten fresh or dried.

The process of making wine can be described simply: one crushes the ripe grapes, puts them into a barrel with yeast, allows the yeast to ferment using the sugar from the grapes, and decants the fermented juice into bottles for consumption. But then one must consider all the variables that go into creating not just an alcoholic grape juice, but a clear, aromatic, flavorful wine. That is where winemaking becomes an art.

A household winemaker may cultivate a few rows of grapevines that produce only a few hundred kilos of grapes. But the ratio of grapes to finished wine is almost one to one. So a few hundred kilos of grapes will yield a few hundred kilos of wine. Or, since one kilo is the weight of one liter of wine, a few hundred liters of wine—sufficient to meet a family's annual needs.

At the household level of winemaking, the grapes may be crushed by hand, if few enough, or by foot, as seen in old movies. At the hardware store in Neapoli, one can buy a grape crushing machine. The grapes used to be fermented, aged and transported in barrels of oak, pine or chestnut. Then plastic barrels replaced wood for household use. A backyard shed may serve as the wine *cava*, where the barrels sit in dark, cool shade until the fermented wine is drawn off into glass bottles, or even recycled plastic ones, and refrigerated until consumed.

At the end of August, I was invited to a small farm just outside Neapoli for the grape pressing. Kyrio Psarakis (Mr. Psarakis) grows thirty different varieties of grapes in small plots scattered through his olive grove. All thirty go into his homemade wine. By the time I arrived at nine in the morning, the grapes had been cut and dumped into the *lino*, a square concrete vat with a brass spigot in one corner. A young man wearing rubber boots, Spiro, was walking on the grapes, squashing the juice out of them. Years ago, the *lino* would have been built of stone, but Kyrio Psarakis' concrete *lino* is large and flat-bottomed and easy to clean. When about two inches of juice had accumulated in the bottom of the *lino*, the spigot was opened and grape juice flowed into a plastic bucket. As soon as one bucket filled, Kyrio Psarakis' brother replaced it with another. Meanwhile, Kyrio Psarakis and his grandson, Nikolas, carried the full bucket of juice to his *cava*, a room built on the garden level underneath the house. With Nikolas steadying the screen-bottomed funnel, Kyrio Psarakis poured the juice into the smallest of his three plastic wine barrels.

"This one holds one hundred and twenty kilos," Kyrio Psarakis told me. Gesturing to the other corners of the cool room, he said, "That one holds two hundred and forty kilos

~ *Greece* ~

and the big one, three hundred." That should be plenty of wine for one family, I thought.

He stirred the juice with his hand, keeping the skins from clogging the funnel. When all the juice had flowed into the barrel, he squeezed out the skins and dropped them into another plastic bucket. "For distilling *tsipouro*," he said. "It tastes even better than ouzo."

"How long does the juice take to turn into wine?" I asked.

"Sixty-five days total," he responded. "After it ferments for about thirty days, I put the lid on the barrel very tight and wait another thirty-five days. Then I open this spigot and pour a glass. I taste it. If I am lucky, it tastes very good."

But the wine-pressing did not end with a single trodding. Spiro had shoveled all the skins and twigs into one corner of the *lino*. He put down a bunch of straight branches that reminded me of a large whiskbroom. Then he shoveled some skins onto the branches and covered them with more branches. He stepped heavily on the branches and once more juice flowed out the drain into a plastic bucket. When the trickle slowed, he lifted up the branches and shook out the grape skins, depositing them in another corner of the *lino*. He worked his way down the pile.

While Spiro was finishing with that stage of juice extraction, Kyrio Psarakis was assembling his grape press. This looked like a circle of barrel staves with spaces in between. The staves sat on a large metal saucer with a spout in its lip. A tall screw rose out of the center of the press. Spiro shoveled the remains of the grape skins into the grape press. Kyrio Psarakis packed the skins down tightly with his hands. When about half of the large pile of skins had been stuffed into the press, the lid was fitted on. Then he carefully stacked six wooden blocks on top and began tightening the screw. Slowly, carefully, lest the wooden blocks slip out of position, Kyrio Psarakis and his brother worked the press. A new trickle of grape juice flowed out of the barrel staves into the metal saucer and down into a plastic barrel. When juice stopped flowing, the press was opened and more skins shoveled in.

Nothing was wasted. Every drop of juice made it into the fermenting barrel. The skins were saved to make *tsipouro*. Only sixty-four more days to go until Kyrio Psarakis and his family will be enjoying this year's vintage.

A Step Beyond

Yiannis Vatistas came from a fishing family in the Vatika town of Aghia Marina, close to the remote tip of land that juts out into the sea and is known as Cape Malea. Like every other family, the Vatistas grew grape vines. Yiannis took charge of producing the family wine. But unlike most family wine producers, Yiannis became fascinated working with the vines. He enlarged the family vineyard and experimented with producing more and higher quality wine. His wine became known as the best around. He soon produced enough to be sold at the fish restaurant his family owned in Athens. Then other restaurants began to offer his wine. The more time Yiannis spent in his vineyards, the more he wanted to learn. He began researching the varieties of grapes that had been grown traditionally in Vatika and expanded his plantings to include Asyritiko, Aghiorgytiko and Roditis.

In 1996, he realized he could not do it all. He hired an experienced oenologist, one of the first Greek women oenologists, Mary Flerianou, as his winemaker. Trained first as a mathematician, then as a chemist, Mary contributed not only her chemist's skills, but her aesthetic expertise in the art of winemaking.

By that time, Yiannis had over sixteen hectares of Greek and French varieties of grapes under cultivation. He was no longer producing only taverna-style barrel wine, but had moved into the realm of commercial bottled wines. He blended Chardonnay and Cabernet Sauvignon with local varieties of grapes to produce flavorful white and red table wines.

Mary joined Yiannis after working at another Greek winery for eight years. She had developed her own philosophy about the best potential for Greek wines. She pushed Yiannis to go back to his roots and refocus on the local Greek varieties, believing that that is where Greek wines can enjoy a competitive advantage in the world market place. And so Yiannis planted Petroulianos, Kydonitsa, Athiri, Monemvasia, Malvazia, Malagouzia, Thrapsa, and Mavroudi.

As a team, Mary and Yiannis continued to expand the market for Vatistas wines. And Yiannis continued to expand his vineyards. Moving along the Vatika coast to the west, he planted ten hectares of vineyards below the town of Pandanasas, on hillsides just above the sea. He also established vineyards farther north along the peninsula, near Monemvasia.

With seven years of experience, Yiannis began to enter Vatistas wines in international competitions. The medals began to accumulate: bronze in Thessaloniki 2001; two silvers in Brussels 2001; silver in Thessaloniki 2004; gold and silver in Brussels 2004; silver in Thessaloniki 2005; Gran Menzione in Vinitaly 2006; and special recognition in Japan 2006.

Mary's vision proved correct. The wines winning the top international prizes were Assyrtiko, Kydonitsa, Vatistas Cabernet/Aghiorghitiko, Petroulianos, Red Regional wine of Monemvasia and Fume. The vines of Vatika are proving as resilient and vital as the now-restored fortress of Monemvasia.

While Yiannis Vatistas has become the major commercial winemaker in Vatika, nearly every extended family continues to proudly produce wine of its own. The spirit of Dionysus is alive. Wine is an intrinsic part of life in Vatika, whether one is a household winemaker, or simply someone who appreciates the final product.

"Dionysus' body was torn apart each winter," Thanasis concluded, "Then reborn each spring." Every year, grapevines sprout new shoots, leaves, flowers that become grapes. The grapes are duly harvested and transformed into wine. The wine that was a crucial part of Dionysian celebrations is enjoyed by inhabitants and modern-day voyagers alike.

Pathway to Paradise

~

We were heading for *Paradisi*—Paradise. Remnants of raindrops dripped from the eucalyptus trees as we started walking. My daughter Piper and I had spent all day indoors, confined by rain and wind. Now, late afternoon, a window of opportunity appeared. The rain stopped; the wind died down. Closing the black iron gate behind us, we turned right and headed upstream. That is, our imprecise instructions were to walk in the dry riverbed underneath the first bridge, then head up. There was nothing natural about this riverbed. It had been paved in concrete, and the banks were not crumbling earth, but solid stonework.

We skirted puddles that had accumulated in concrete depressions. A car was parked in the riverbed under the bridge, a substitute carport. Clearly flash floods were not expected here. A narrow path led from the riverbed up to the street. Was that our route? We had no map or hand-drawn chart, just a few verbal instructions. We walked a bit further, discovered a large side creek entering our riverbed and returned to the narrow path. As we climbed the short pitch, our running shoes clung to the mud.

Piper spotted the symbol: a red circle inside a white square. That must mean we were on the hiking trail. Or at least *a* hiking trail. In fact, we were back on the paved road. Why had we bothered to walk in the riverbed when we could have just walked up the road? We had simply followed instructions, with no understanding of the geography. Now we see through the mirror dimly.

Apple trees blossomed along both sides of the road. Without realizing it, we had left Neapolis and were walking uphill through the countryside. Houses spaced out, surrounded by olive trees, a few fig trees, roses beginning to bloom.

Piper strode purposefully, her long legs carrying her at a pace I could barely maintain. She is three inches taller than I am. She is stronger, too.

Twenty years ago, I carried her on my back, a baby in an aluminum-framed carrier with a canvas seat. During a long hike, sometimes she would fall asleep, her head bobbing against the back of my neck. Other times, she would get impatient with her means of conveyance. She would stand on the aluminum crossbar and pull my hair. White blond ringlets have turned to dark blond waves of shoulder-length hair. Her blue eyes still sparkle with mischief. But today the mischief is tempered with a degree of understanding.

A dog barked at us. We looked down into a yard of deep, churned mud. The dog was standing in the only dry place —on the side of a twenty-gallon metal drum. The drum was lying on its side in the mud and had been opened at one end to create a crude doghouse. The dog was chained to the barrel. The chain clanged as he struggled to maintain his balance, to keep from slipping off the rounded barrel side. His barks sounded like cries for help. But there was nothing we could do.

~ Greece ~

The hillsides around Neapolis appear sparsely vegetated, until one walks through them. Rough bushes and high weeds force one to stick to a path. But there are many paths to choose from in Vatika. Some of them follow dirt roads that turn into tracks. And some of them disappear completely, from lack of regular maintenance. I had seen trail symbols painted on rocks along the way to Mesochori, Faraklo, Aghia Paraskevi and La. Not so many years ago, donkeys laden with supplies plied up and down the rocky paths, crisscrossing the countryside.

After a mile or so, we came to an intersection. A dirt track turned off to the left, while the paved road continued. We saw our first trail sign: a stick-bodied hiker with a backpack and a walking stick on a small red placard. It read 3 *Paradisi* 2.8 km. So we were on trail number 3 and we were on the right track! We turned left.

Within two minutes we stood befuddled. We had walked out of civilization, past the country houses with their wide gardens. We were in the midst of an untamed landscape. The track petered out in an olive grove. A streambed coming down the hillside seemed to be the only route. Would the walking route to Paradise follow a streambed?

Why not? Are there not four rivers in the gardens of Paradise? They flow with wine, water, milk and honey. The fountain of everlasting life is where they converge in the center of the garden. I have heard that is the description of Paradise in the Koran. And the charbagh gardens of Moghul India are laid out according to that design. Piper and I could not tell which of the four rivers we were in. Although the bed was wide, filled with smooth, worn stones, it was empty.

Around a bend, we came upon a square stone house. Two rows of olive trees stood like sentinels, marking this small plot of a former home. The stone terraces were intact, but, though the house appeared solid, the roof was gone. The doors and window frames gaped open, empty. Where had the residents gone?

I imagined myself living in that house. I could see the roof covered in red tiles with upturned corners. The window and doorframes, the door and wooden shutters were painted deep ocean blue. I imagined laboring with my husband building those stone terraces—one rock at a time. The rocks were heavy. Each one had to be carried from the field to the wall, then lifted into place, then worked into the final scheme. As we worked, we were drenched in sweat. It poured down my face, along my neck. But carrying a heavy stone, I couldn't wipe away the sweat. It stung my eyes. Course by course, we built the terrace wall.

Three terraces rose above the creek bed. I knew what labor and love had gone into building each one of them. I saw the fruit trees planted close to the house, the olive grove spread out along the terraces.

I imagined myself sitting on the doorstep, deciding where to plant the lemon trees, the pear trees. I chose an especially sunny spot for the fig tree. Outside the kitchen door, I planted herbs—mint and oregano. We built an arbor for the grape vines, establishing a spot to sit in the shade.

My dream ended. As Piper and I walked past the homestead, it returned to its actual condition, abandoned and left to ruin.

The streambed twisted and turned. The trail symbol, the red circle in a white square, was painted on a rock here, a stone wall there.

~ *Greece* ~

We passed another abandoned homestead, then another. A metal pipe crossed the dry streambed, spanning from one bank to the other, well above our heads. Water sprayed from a leak in a pipe joint. That was where the water in the stream had gone! Somewhere above us, the stream had been diverted into a pipe. Presumably, the pipe carried the water to a point where it was put to use. Maybe it was being used to irrigate the olive groves that still populated the multiple terraces.

After we passed under the pipe with its artificial waterfall, the streambed became more difficult to negotiate. We jumped from boulder to boulder, continuing our ascent. I followed Piper's lead, giving thanks I could.

A week earlier, Piper had been on her spring break from the American University in Cairo where she was studying for a semester. She and a group of friends had traveled in backpacking, hostelling, student style from Egypt to Jordan, then into Israel to visit Tel Aviv and Jerusalem. I had expressed concern when she told me of their plans to go into Israel. The chronic terrorist attacks against unarmed civilians claim so many victims there. I could not bear for her to be among them. She emailed from Jerusalem to tell us that she and her friends had left the bus station in Tel Aviv twenty-four hours before it was bombed. Eight people died.

After several days in Jerusalem, she and her friends tried to enter Syria, but were turned back. They retraced their route through Jordan and into Egypt and decided to relax for a couple of days at the seaside resort of Dahab. On the day of their departure from Dahab, there were two busses to Cairo, one at 2:30 p.m. and one at 10:00 at night. Piper was inclined to take the night bus, but her friends preferred to get back to their dorm at a reasonable hour. So the group left Dahab in the afternoon. At 7 p.m. that evening, three bombs exploded in Dahab, one at the restaurant where Piper and her friends had eaten the day before and would have probably eaten again that evening. Twenty-three people died in the blasts.

Piper had come to Greece for the final days of her spring break to spend time with me in a secure environment. There are no guarantees of safety anywhere, but Piper had been spared twice, by increasingly narrow margins. In'ch Allah, God willing, I was clambering over boulders, hiking behind her up a streambed in Vatika.

A trail sign indicated a right turn, out of the streambed onto a narrow path through a weed-choked field. Again we passed stone terraces, still planted in olive trees, then a roofless stone house. A short flight of concrete stairs took us to a paved road. Red placards with stick-figured hikers directed us to Faraklo in one direction, or back the way we had come to Neapolis.

It started to rain. Piper and I stood under a broad-leafed mulberry tree and shared some almonds I had carried in my pocket. We had arrived in Paradise—the olive trees, the stone house next to the creek, the grape vines, looked exactly like those in Neapolis, where we had begun. Why had we made the effort to hike here? The only difference from where we had started was the perspective. At a higher elevation, we enjoyed a more expansive view.

In a flash, I understood: Paradise is not an ultimate destination. There is nothing in Paradise that we do not already have; there is nothing to look forward to. Paradise is wherever we find ourselves, here and now, today.

Cultivating Olives

~

"All set to go then, dear?" the burly, bearded Greek taxi driver cheerfully called out to me in broad Australian. Yiannis is a native-born Greek, but he spent from ages eight to eighteen in Australia. When he returned to Greece as a young man, he decided to stay. He is a member of the Greek diaspora: Greeks who have spent a few years, or whose families have spent a generation or two, living abroad, but who ultimately return to this dry, rock-strewn mountainous land.

Appearances are deceiving. Yiannis only drives his taxi when he is not tending his groves of olives: one thousand trees in five separate plots around Neapoli. Yiannis is an olive grower disguised as a taxi driver. For five hours, as he drove expertly, speedily through Sparta, Tripoli and Corinth to Athens, he talked about his olive trees, harvesting his crop, and the cooperative olive oil press.

In a way, Yiannis was telling me a familiar tale. My father was a grower. He was born in Holland, where his family had a market garden and grew vegetables under Dutch lights and in greenhouses. After he emigrated to the United States at the age of twenty-three, he worked on a farm, then started his own plant nursery. Eventually, he built eleven acres of greenhouses and grew carnations and roses commercially. He sold his flowers through a wholesalers' cooperative. I identified with Yiannis' stories about weather, pests, and marketing his crop.

Farming runs in families. Yiannis inherited his olive trees from his father. His plots are separated because over time a family's land is divided between children, then transferred between relatives, until what any one person owns is a hodgepodge of small properties. Having a five-piece farm is inefficient. Yiannis described the difficulties, "I have to drive between them, so time I could be working, I am on the road, traveling from one plot to another. I have to have five buildings for tools and equipment. If I don't want to carry all my tools with me, I have to have five different sets."

Small and large olive groves form silver-leaved patches in the landscape quilt of Vatika. But the hundreds of thousands of olive trees that thrive in Greece are not native species. There are several theories about their origins. Some scientists believe olive trees originated in Asia Minor; other scientists claim they originated in the Caucasus Mountains. Olive trees appear to have spread over time from Syria towards Greece by way of Anatolia. By the sixteenth century BCE, the Phoenicians spread olive trees throughout the Greek islands. By the twelfth century BCE, olive trees were growing on the Greek mainland. By the fourth century BCE, the importance of olive cultivation had increased to a point that Solon issued decrees regulating the planting of olive trees.

Olive trees married happily into the local soil and climactic conditions. The so-called Mediterranean climate exists in only a few places in the world outside the basin of the Mediterranean Sea: the west coast of Australia, the west coast of South Africa and the west coast of the United States around San Francisco Bay. It is characterized by cool, rainy winters, and hot, dry summers. In a Mediterranean climate, one must plant in the fall to take advantage of the rainy season. Plants planted in late spring will suffer from the immediate stress of the summer drought. Transplants must be planted with these conditions in mind.

I, too, am a transplant here. In my life, I have moved many times. As a Foreign Service officer, I moved with my husband and two daughters from Colorado to Washington, D.C., to Guangzhou, China, back to Washington, D.C., and to Paris, France. Then my family tired of moving and we settled near my husband's family outside San Francisco. Now our children are grown. My husband has returned to his roots in Marin County. But I have never felt at home there. When we lived in Paris, I discovered I prefer to live in Europe. Now in Greece, I have found a location that suits me. Cities and towns alike are characterized by neighborhoods. Virtually everything one needs can be found within walking distance. I have found an intellectual climate conducive to creativity and a physical climate conducive to health. In Neapoli, I write every morning and swim in the clear, cool Aegean every afternoon. Locals enjoy their *banio*, or daily swim, before a mid-afternoon meal and *mesimeri*, a late afternoon nap. Evenings are for visiting with friends and late dinners under the stars. Like the olive trees, I have found a climate where I can thrive.

Olive trees are now an inherent part of Greek culture and cuisine. Whenever oil is needed in cooking, olive oil is used, from deep-frying french-fries, to oil-and-lemon fish sauce to tangy salad dressings. According to Sylvia, mother of three, a Greek family of five uses approximately one hundred and twenty kilos of olive oil each year. That translates into one hundred and thirty-three liters, or over two liters of olive oil per person per month. Olive oil is used in soap and soothing lotions. The curved-grained wood is used to fashion items from kitchen utensils to furniture.

Most every family in Vatika has a few olive trees. They may be grown on a terrace outside the front door, or on an inherited piece of property known only to initiates. When the olives are ripe, the branches can be combed with rakes and olives will drop onto a cloth placed beneath the trees. The best olives are saved for the table. They are washed, then slit open, so the salt and vinegar brine they are placed in can penetrate and preserve them. After several days, they can be removed from the brine, covered in olive oil and refrigerated. Other more sophisticated recipes include drying the brine-preserved olives with aromatic herbs.

The rest of the olives from a family's trees are taken to the local coop. The traditional olive press in Kriovrissis on the hillside above Neapoli consisted of two stones turned by donkeys harnessed in traces. The building still stands, but the millstones are gone. The olive press in use today is located in Pandanasus. Its stainless steel presses are powered by electricity. But the outcome is the same: kilos of green-gold olive oil.

I, too, have a product emerging from my time in Greece: writing. First, essays on gardening in the now-familiar Mediterranean climate, but in a place far-removed from San Francisco Bay. Then a screenplay I had thought of for years, but never written down, followed by an anthology of essays by writers, all inspired by the same climate, during our workshop in Vatika. What is it about this environment, one that appears so rocky and desolate, yet results in such fecundity?

When a family takes its bounty of olives to the cooperative press, the olives are weighed. For every kilo weighed in, the family receives a certain amount of oil in return, minus a commission of oil paid to the cooperative for its services.

A commercial grower like Yiannis does the same thing. He takes his harvested olives to the press to be weighed then transformed into oil. But rather than taking his oil home, the cooperative credits the grower with a certain number of kilos to be sold. The oil is sold at auction. Buyers are an international crowd. Some come from Italy. These buyers are commercial olive oil producers themselves who buy the rich Greek oil to add flavor to the lighter Italian oil. According to Yiannis, the Italians use a ratio of one part Greek oil to nine parts Italian oil to achieve the flavor they desire. The oil is marketed as Italian oil, though it has been flavor-enhanced.

"Considering we produce the best olive oil, we don't make as much money as we should," Yiannis complained.

I commiserated with him. "I think it's a marketing problem. Greek olive oil could be marketed as the highest end olive oil, so rich in flavor you only need to add a little bit to your salads to get fantastic taste. You should be getting a premium price for your oil. But, of course, that would require a whole marketing campaign. And who would pay for it? The coop?" I asked.

"Not bloody likely," came the response.

Another local olive grower, Kosta, was kind enough to take me to visit his olive grove. Kosta also has a day job: a thriving practice as a physical therapist. He took me to his family's farm where he cultivates almost nine hundred olive trees. In some of his groves, one-inch diameter black plastic pipes festooned the trees, stretching from the branches of one tree to the next. "What are those pipes for?" I asked.

"Irrigation," Kosta explained. He took me to the pump house for the well his father drilled. He poured twenty liters of diesel fuel into the engine that powers the pump. He added water to the radiator, then checked the oil. He turned the pump engine on, then opened the valves on four-inch black plastic pipes that carried the water to the smaller pipes hanging from the trees.

In some sections of Kosta's olive grove, the plastic pipes run along the ground, just as they do in my garden in California. The olive trees can obviously survive without irrigation, but with some added water they will increase their yield.

"When is the olive harvest?" I asked.

"In the fall," Kosta replied. "Usually mid-October. We have a saying here that when the olives are yellow, they are ready to pick. But I also have a few trees of Kalamata olives for the table. Those olives aren't ripe until they are black. Olive trees bloom in late April. When the trees are blooming, they look white instead of green. The fruit sets in early summer. Then, of course, pests may attack, especially flies. We call them *dakos*. The flies lay their eggs in the young olives, then when the eggs hatch, the larvae eat the olives from the inside." He searched a tree for an infected olive. He showed me the black spot on the outside of the olive that indicated a fly had laid its eggs there. He opened the olive with his fingernail and traced the path of the larvae.

~ Greece ~

"What can you do about that?" I asked.

"First, we hang traps in the trees. See those plastic bottles hanging from the branches?"

I saw gallon-size white plastic bottles hanging from occasional trees.

"Those contain a pheromone that attracts the flies. They fly into the bottle and drown. But the bottles are just indicators of the fly population. If I find more than ten drowned flies, then I have to spray the trees with insecticide. If I find just a few flies in the bottle, I know there will be some damage to the crop, but I can tolerate that. I prefer not to spray."

"After the harvest, I put my trees to bed," Kosta continued. "I prune out dead branches and crossing branches and generally shape the trees. Then I mulch around the base of the trunks. So next year we can start all over again."

Turtle Tracks

~

The loggerhead turtle swam slowly toward the shore. Moonlight reflected on the surface of the sea, so brightly it outshone the stars. As the turtle reached the sand, she used her paddle arms to push her way onto the beach. Her paddle legs pushed against the sand. With great effort, she climbed across the hard, wet sand until she reached the softer, dry sand. She kept going. How far would the water rise with the tide? How far up would waves splash when pushed by a south wind? She climbed further, until she decided her eggs would be safe. Then she started to dig. With her paddle arms, she moved kilos and kilos of sand. When her nest hole was about a meter deep, she positioned herself so her eggs would drop into the deepest part of the hole. Finally, she was able to relax and deposit almost one hundred eggs. When she finished, she had to get to work again. She covered the eggs with the sand she had scraped from the hole. When she finished, there was still a slight depression in the sand. She headed back to the sea, creating a new track. As she pushed one paddle arm, then the other, then each paddle leg, through the sand, the sky lightened. Soon it would be dawn.

~ *Greece* ~

I begin my beach walk at about nine a.m. I would have liked to start earlier, before the sun hit the sand, but at least I had made it. Twice a week, I walk the same stretch of beach, from the ferry terminal for the island of Elafonisos to Mangano Beach Bar. I am looking for sea turtle tracks, which indicate a new loggerhead turtle nest. From May through August, loggerhead turtles, *Caretta caretta*, return to the beaches all around Vatika Bay and the Myrtoon Sea to lay their eggs. Once every three or four years, a mother turtle will return to the place where she herself was born.

For the past five years, as a volunteer for the local non-governmental organization Toulipa Goulymi, I have walked this same stretch of beach, searching for turtle tracks. Toulipa Goulymi has been recording the turtle nests along the beaches—and the hatchlings—since 2014.

As the number of volunteers increased, and volunteers regularly walked more beaches, more and more nests have been identified. All together, we identified over two hundred turtle nests on local beaches in 2018. ARCHELON, the sea turtle protection organization of Greece, has added Vatika Bay to its map of documented loggerhead nesting sites in Greece.

ARCHELON trained two leaders of Toulipa Goulymi, Yiannis and Maria, to open the nests and confirm that they held eggs. A mother turtle may prepare a nest and be unable to lay eggs in it. She covers it as though it is full, returns to the sea, and may return the next night and build another nest. Yiannis and Maria try to open each nest that has been reported.

As a volunteer, I have participated in opening a nest—but only to the point of digging out the heaviest part of the sand and taking measurements. We start by deciding where the eggs are most likely to be. Then we use our hands, just as the mother turtle used her flippers, digging up kilos and kilos of sand until our arms ache. As soon as we see the tops of the translucent, ping pong ball-sized eggs, Yiannis and Maria take over, gently dusting the sand from the fragile eggs. We note the nest's geographical location, its latitude and longitude, its width and depth, and distance from the sea. In exceptional cases, when the nest is too close to the sea, and risks being inundated, Yiannis and Maria dig a new nest farther from the sea, and move the eggs to a safe location. Once all the measurements have been recorded, we push all the sand back over the eggs. We position a wide-meshed metal screen over the nest to protect the eggs from digging dogs, foxes and other predators. Then we build a fence of sticks, or place a metal cage over the nest, along with a printed notice that this is the nest of the endangered species of sea turtle *Caretta caretta*, and thus protected under European law.

About two months later, volunteers begin monitoring the turtle hatch. But the hatching may not start until after ten at night—or even later—and not be complete for hours. Who can do this work night after night during hatching season? Very few. I have only watched one night-time hatch. The nest was on the beach right in front of the largest hotel in Neapolis. After eating dinner in town, I received a text message from Maria, telling me where to go. She and several grade-school students were already there monitoring the situation. I knelt down in the sand and joined them.

The two-inch long hatchlings were just digging their way up through the sand. They pushed and scrambled

~ *Greece* ~

against each other to reach air to breathe. Then they began their perilous journey to the sea. Our job that night was to create a corridor for the hatchlings and make sure they reached the sea. Using strips of fabric attached to bamboo stakes, we marked the edges of the hatchlings' path to the sea. It is essential that each hatchling makes the journey on its own: it must imprint the way to the sea in its brain, so it can return to the same location when it is fully mature.

Of the approximately one hundred eggs the mother turtle laid, about eighty will hatch. Of those eighty, only half—about forty—will make it to the water. They are born knowing that they must seek the moonlight reflecting on the surface of the sea. Thus, turtle hatchlings automatically head toward the brightest light. Along undeveloped beaches, like the one I walk from Pounta to Mangano, there are no competing sources of light. However, turtles hatching on the beaches of the town of Neapolis, or near the road in Limnes, are easily confused. Lights from the restaurants and hotels outshine the moon. Streetlights are full moons in fatal disguise.

Having finally made it to the sea, the hatchling turtles are the object of many predators. For protection, they may hide in Sargasso weed or other floating plants or debris. Within a few years, only a fraction of the forty turtles that made it to the sea are still alive. The odds of survival are so poor that only one in a thousand eggs will live to become a mature turtle able to reproduce. Out of ten nests of one hundred eggs each, only one turtle will actually return to the beach where it was born.

I recall these odds of survival every time I walk this beach. I carry a large plastic trash bag with me. The primary purpose of my walk is to look for fresh turtle tracks, but the secondary reason is to pick up trash that accumulates here. Some of the trash is heedlessly dropped by visitors to the beach: plastic cups, plastic straws, plastic bags, plastic mesh, cigarette lighters, butts and filters. Other trash is washed in from the sea: lengths of cord, fishing line, smoke flares, plastic glow sticks, and tiny—and tinier— pieces of plastic. All of these pieces of trash are potential turtle killers. The dead turtle found most recently on the beach was strangled by a plastic bag. Not long ago, another dead turtle was found with no marks of violence. Perhaps, weighted down by the many pieces of indigestible plastic it had eaten, it was unable to come to the surface to breathe, and drowned.

In the past three years, seventy-six dead turtles have been found on the beaches of Vatika Bay and the Myrtoon Sea. These dead turtles represent seven hundred and sixty turtle nests, seventy-six thousand turtle eggs. Most of the dead turtles bear signs of deliberate aggression, most often smashed heads. Others have carapaces cut to pieces by propellers. Who is responsible for killing these rare, endangered creatures? The knee-jerk response is "Fishermen." Turtles may become entangled in fishing nets, damaging the nets and potentially eating the catch. Greek fishermen have yet to adopt fishing nets with turtle-excluder devices. Sea turtles may be viewed by fishermen as competitors for the limited source of the fishermen's livelihood. Some turtles may be killed out of pure malice.

How can local attitudes toward sea turtles be changed? Education—awareness raising—is the answer. So Yiannis visits several school classrooms each year with a slide show presentation. Elementary school students from Monemvasia have painted signs which were posted on beaches

~ Greece ~

where turtles nest. Toulipa Goulymi organizes beach cleanup walks, and parents bring their children. Other volunteers like me walk the beaches wearing our T-shirts from ARCHELON or Toulipa Goulymi, so that everyone who sees us is reminded once again that turtles must be protected. At the first Pavlopetri Eco-Marine Film Festival held in July 2019, two films dealt with sea turtles: one a winner of the International Ocean Film Festival's 2019 Student Film Competition entitled *Turtle Crisis*, the other a full-length documentary entitled *A Plastic Ocean*. After the screening of *A Plastic Ocean*, two teachers approached one of the Festival organizers. They said they wanted every school child in Neapolis to see that film.

Local attitudes toward sea turtles lag behind international recognition: In April 2017, Mission Blue, the prestigious international marine protection organization, designated Vatika Bay and the Myrtoon Sea as the first Hope Spot in Greece. Mission Blue made its designation based on the iconic species that inhabit Vatika Bay—whales, dolphins, monk seals and loggerhead turtles—in proximity to the submerged archeological site of Pavlopetri.

From where I am, about four kilometers from the ferry terminal and Pavlopetri, I can see Mangano Beach Bar half a kilometer ahead. And I see the distinctive tracks of a turtle etched in the wet sand. Last night, a mother turtle was here! Her tail has left a mark like a knife, cutting a trail. As I get closer, I can see the scoops of sand taken by each of her paddle arms and legs. The tracks head upwards into the sand dunes. I am amazed she travelled so far uphill. I see the depression in the sand where she has dug her nest and then covered it. And I see where she headed back to the sea, leaving a parallel set of tracks. The incoming tide is already washing away the tracks in the hard sand. In a few hours, the wind will blow loose sand into the tracks, leaving them indistinguishable from other irregularities. For thousands of years, this camouflage worked in favor of the turtle hatchlings, rendering the nest nearly invisible. Today, with threats from humans on the rise, the sea turtles can use all the help we can give. I take photos of the tracks and nest area and send them to Maria. Then I gather some sticks and mark the nest so Yiannis and Maria can come and open it. I am bursting with this news. I want to celebrate this small victory.

    I continue my walk, picking up pieces of plastic trash, and I look out at the Bay. Somewhere out there, there is a small head breaking the surface of the water, taking a deep breath, and diving down, slowly swimming into the open sea.

Eternal Pavlopetri

~

The sailors breathed a sigh of relief as they rounded Cape Malea, and the wind shifted to the south. It would be clear sailing now to the port town of Pavlopetri. The hills of Elafonisos were clearly visible on their left. The mountainous northern boundary of the Bay rose on their right. All they had to do was steer straight to the end of the long, narrow bay to the sandy beaching area at its western end. Cape Malea was notorious for its storms and conflicting currents. At the point where the Ionian Sea meets the Aegean Sea, sailors often encountered challenging conditions. But today the weather had cooperated, and they would soon reach their home port.

It had been a successful voyage. They had traded the textiles woven in Pavlopetri for some lovely pottery. They had acquired a new venerable icon for the temple: a small beautifully crafted figurine of a goddess. Their voyage had taken them to Crete, where they had observed the powerful—and intrusive—Minoan government of Knossos in action, another reason to be happy to be heading home to their independent city.

Each sailor dreamed of that evening's celebration. For some, it would be coming home to his own family: a chance to be surrounded by his wife and children. Others were returning to their parents' homes. For the captain and the navigator, the celebration would be an official welcome from the mayor of Pavlopetri, also leader of the surrounding agricultural region.

In 2,500 BCE, when the sailors reached their homes at Pavlopetri, the town covered about eight hectares of land. It comprised one- and two-story buildings of adobe walls built on stone foundations. Streets of houses were built around courtyards, and a large administrative center dominated the town. Warehouses stockpiled terra cotta pithoi filled with olives, olive oil, grain, wine and honey.

As I walk along the beach today, I dream of those ancient mariners. On the hills overlooking the Bay, sheep and goats graze on grasses and short shrubs, just as they did 4,500 years ago. Olive trees and grapevines, cotton, wheat, onions and other vegetables, all grow well in the soil near Pavlopetri. Buyers from Spain and Italy purchase local olive oil to add flavor to their milder oil. Farmers still grow onions and other vegetables. They tend honey bees, gather honey and ferment mead. They harvest their grapes and ferment wine. The olives and olive oil, garden vegetables, honey and wine that I consume today, all link me with the people who lived in Pavlopetri.

These days, Pavlopetri is submerged in two to three meters of water. It sank gradually, at the rate of about one meter every thousand years, and by 1,000 BCE, Pavlopetri had disappeared. Fifteen hundred years is a long time for a port to survive and develop. From a navigational standpoint, it had an extremely favorable location. It was undoubtedly a very important port town. The foundations of the streets,

~ Greece ~

courtyards and buildings, as well as the thousands of findings archeologists have uncovered, reveal the story. Hundreds of loom weights tell of a thriving textile production; pottery shards from Thessaloniki, Crete, Sicily and Cyprus indicate trade routes; a bronze goddess figurine speaks of religion.

From the time Pavlopetri disappeared in 1,000 BCE until recent times, the significance of the submerged ruins was unrecognized. Local people knew that something had been located there, and nearly everyone had pottery fragments from the site in their homes.

In 1967, Dr. Nicholas Flemming was travelling through the Peloponnese, looking for ancient port sites. He had nothing but his understanding of sailing and navigation to guide him. When he saw Vatika Bay, he thought what a marvelous protected area existed at the western end of the Bay. He took his snorkeling and aqualung gear and checked it out. What he found, amazed him. He used a measuring stick to create a basic map of the ruins. His observation and logic had led him to an archeological site of large dimensions.

In 1968, a team from Cambridge University, led by Dr. Anthony Harding, came to Pavlopetri to map the site. They discovered even more foundations, and added to Flemming's map.

Separately, Dr. Aggelos Delavorias of the Greek Ministry of Culture's Department of Lakonian Antiquities came to Neapolis on a gathering mission. He went from house to house asking the local inhabitants if they had any pieces of pottery or other items they had gathered from the western end of Vatika Bay, now recognized as the archeological site of Pavlopetri. He gathered wheelbarrows full of pottery. The Municipality of Neapolis offered to store the huge number of items until the Ministry of Culture could receive them. Over generations, the site had been very effectively cleaned—looted of surface artifacts. Dr. Delacovias' collection of findings from Pavlopetri is now stored at the Ministry of Culture in Athens.

After the initial excitement of Flemming's discovery, nothing happened at Pavlopetri for the next forty years. In 2009, the Ministry of Culture awarded a five-year permit for the excavation and mapping of Pavlopetri to the University of Nottingham. The team, led by Dr. Jon Henderson and Dr. Chrysanthi Gallou, in cooperation with Dr. Elias Spondilis of the Ministry of Culture's Department of Underwater Antiquities, brought an international group of scientists to Pavlopetri. The University of Sydney's contingent, led by Dr. Oscar Pizarro, was responsible for photographing Pavlopetri, using the most up-to-date techniques. Their Unmanned Robotic Vehicle photographed Pavlopetri in stereoscope and transmitted the images directly to the computers of the scientists headquartered at the local Greek taverna nearby. Dr. Nicholas Flemming joined the group.

Simultaneously, the Hellenic Center for Marine Research, under the direction of Dr. Dimitris Sakellariou, carried out a study of the sea floor of Vatika Bay. The geologists from HCMR were looking at the potential reason for the submersion of the ancient port. The question was: did the sea level rise, or did the sea floor sink? The geologists' answer is that the total submergence of five meters was caused by both processes together. The sea floor gradually sank about two meters, as the tectonic plates located to the east of Vatika Bay slowly, slowly shifted in relation to each other. In addition to the tectonic subsidence, melting of the ice caps after the Ice Age caused a further inundation of about three meters depth.

That gradual inundation also turned Elafonisos into an island. In 1967, when Flemming arrived on the scene, Elafonisos was an island, although as recently as 2,000 years ago, it was connected to the mainland. The stone outcroppings that barely rise above the surface of the Bay just north of the islet of Pavlopetri were part of a ridge that protected the city from the south winds. The two large chamber tombs, which one can now swim into, were dug into the ridge. Boats would have entered the port of Pavlopetri from the south, beaching on the smooth sands of Pounta Beach.

Dr. Oscar Pizarro of the University of Sydney and Dr. Jon Henderson of the University of Nottingham quickly published the results of their sophisticated photography and mapping work. Major buildings had been discovered and a whole new section of the town had been revealed. The photographic images produced by the University of Sydney have been used to create stone-by-stone three-dimensional reconstructions of individual building foundations. The University of Nottingham has yet to publish information on the excavated findings, which include at least one bronze figurine, hundreds of loom weights and thousands of pot shards. According to its permit, it has ten years from the end of the permit in which to do so, which will be in 2024.

Scientists identified the largest threats to the preservation and protection of Pavlopetri as shifting sediments, anchoring and fishing by small boats at the site, pollution, and looting. To assist the Ministry of Culture in coping with these problems, the U.S. non-profit organization the Alliance for the Restoration of Cultural Heritage, through its Greek Chapter, raised the money to purchase eleven buoys, which were donated to the Ministry of Culture. In 2016, during the first Pavlopetri Watch Day, an event supported by the World Monuments Fund to raise awareness about Pavlopetri, Dr. Aggeliki Simosi, Director of the Department of Underwater Antiquities, placed the buoys around the perimeter of the site. Dr. Nicholas Flemming attended the ceremony, which was conducted on a traditional wooden boat, a caique. The concept was to alert small boats to the existence of the archeological site and warn them to keep out of it. In less than one year, all the buoys had disappeared. Greek ARCH replaced them with much cheaper buoys, which also quickly disappeared. The Ministry of Culture gave up on that idea.

The threat of pollution to the existing ruins comes from two sources: the large commercial ships that anchor in Vatika Bay, and runoff of fungicides and pesticides used by local farmers. There is no Special Port Regulation (SPR) governing Vatika Bay. A proposed SPR allowing an unlimited number of ships to anchor in the Bay encountered the outrage of all the hotel owners, restaurants, bars, and cafes that make their living from the sustainable coastal tourism economy. That plan was shelved. Another plan, proposed by a former head of the Coast Guard in Neapolis would limit the number of ships anchored in a very specific part of the Bay to two ships a day during nine months of the year and no ships during June, July, and August; limit the activities the ships could carry out while in the Bay; and limit the length of stay to two days. That SPR, although enjoying the support of the majority of the local population, has yet to be approved.

~ Greece ~

In 2017, the Ministry of Culture delineated the boundaries of the Pavlopetri archeological site and in February 2018, they were published in the official Greek government gazette, called the F.E.K. Based on that publication, the Greek Coast Guard and the Hydrological Service collaborated in having the boundaries of the Pavlopetri archeological site included on all official marine charts. This was the first time a Greek underwater archeological site had appeared on a marine chart.

In 2019, during Pavlopetri Watch Day, the Ministry of Culture presented its proposed Management Plan for Pavlopetri. It includes signage, a designated parking area, wooden walkways to protect the fragile sand dune ecosystem, and an informational kiosk. Interagency consultations regarding the Management Plan are scheduled for fall 2019.

The Greek Coast Guard, which has a station in Neapolis, has been given authority to monitor the coastal area included in the boundaries of the Pavlopetri archeological site. Camping is illegal in Greek archeological sites. The Coast Guard has succeeded in shooing away many of the trailers overnighting in the site.

As of 2019, there are four signs on the highway pointing the way to Pavlopetri. There are no signs at the site itself.

At each of the four Pavlopetri Watch Days 2016-2019, guided snorkeling tours led by the Ministry of Culture have attracted dozens of participants. There is great interest in the site from tourists and locals alike. But there is no way for tourists to identify or understand what the rows of carefully placed submerged stones mean.

What does the future hold for Pavlopetri? The Ministry of Culture has made it clear that it does not intend to authorize further excavation of the site. This is consistent with the philosophy that excavation inevitably destroys a site at the same time it discovers more about it. Some sites must be left for future generations of archeologists to explore. The existing ruins are easily accessible, but require explanation and interpretation in order to be appreciated by tourists. The Ministry of Culture has proposed creating a self-guided tour with laminated maps and a few signed locations. This could also be accomplished via virtual tours that visitors could view online before they begin snorkeling. Before any development starts, there is an opportunity to create a nearly unspoiled site by limiting vehicle access all along the beach from Pounta to Mangano—the full length of the coastline of the designated archeological site. With appropriate care, Pavlopetri could become an important tourist attraction, bolstering the coastal tourism economy, and sparking the imagination of every child and adult who snorkels over the foundations of streets, courtyards and homes.

I would like to know more about the people who lived in Pavlopetri. As I snorkel over the ruins of their homes, I feel the relief of a sailor when he beaches his boat, walks up the street and crosses the lintel into his house. I feel the loss of the parents who buried their baby in a cist grave in a wall. I feel the bustle of the marketplace, the rhythm of working at a loom, the tedium of a warehouse clerk keeping track of pithoi full of olives and grain. There is much we do not know about the lives of the people who lived in Pavlopetri, and much is left to discover. However, one thing I do know: our lives are interconnected, fundamentally the same, and when I swim above Pavlopetri, when I ponder its success,

~ Greece ~

demise, and preservation, the centuries disappear, and I am focused in that unique place that links me to other people, other times.

Story Sources

~

"Unanticipated Snow Cave" first appeared in the anthology *Sheets to the Wind* in 1998 and subsequently in the anthology *Going Alone* in 2004. Copyright © 1998 by Barbara J. Euser.

"Descent from Mt. Communism" first appeared in the anthology *Danger! True Stories of Trouble and Survival* in 1999. Copyright © 1999 by Barbara J. Euser.

"Trekking with the Tiger" first appeared in *Buzzworm* July/August 1991. Copyright © 1991 by Barbara J. Euser.

"Orphans on top of the World" first appeared in *Common Ground* March/April 2004. Copyright © 2004 by Barbara J. Euser.

"Kerala with Two Girls in Tow" first appeared in *passionfruit* fall 2000. Copyright © 2000 by Barbara J. Euser.

"Reflections on Burning a Cocaine Lab" Copyright © 1992 by Barbara J. Euser.

"Helping out with a Bosnian Election" first appeared in *passionfruit* spring/summer 2001. Copyright © 2001 by Barbara J. Euser.

~ Story Sources ~

"Running the Zagreb Marathon" Copyright © 1996 by Barbara J. Euser.

"Across the Sea" first appeared in *passionfruit* spring 2000 issue. Copyright © 1999 by Barbara J. Euser.

"Singlehanded TransPac" first appeared in the anthology *Solo: On Her Own Adventure* in 2005. Copyright © 2004 by Barbara J. Euser.

"Lurley" first appeared in the antholoby *Floating through France: Life between Locks on the Canal du Midi* in 2005. Copyright © 2005 by Barbara J. Euser.

"Chez Paul" first appeared in the anthology *Floating through France: Life between Locks on the Canal du Midi* in 2005. Copyright © 2005 by Barbara J. Euser.

Winegeese" first appeared in the antholoby *Venturing in Ireland: Search for the Modern Celtic Soul in 2007*. Copyright © 2007 by Barbara J. Euser.

"Pangur Ban" first appeared in the anthology *Venturing in Ireland: Search for the Modern Celtic Soul* in 2007. Copyright © 2007 by Barbara J. Euser.

"Mussels Farming in Taranto" first appeared in the anthology *Venturing in Italy: Travels in Puglia, Land between Two Seas* in 2008. Copyright © 2008 by Barbara J. Euser.

"Magna Graecia" first appeared in the anthology *Venturing in Italy: Travels in Puglia, Land between Two Seas* in 2008. Copyright © 2008 by Barbara J. Euser.

~ Story Sources ~

"Vines of Vatika" first appeared in the anthology *Venturing in Southern Greece: The Vatika Odysseys* in 2006. Copyright © 2006 by Barbara J. Euser.

"Pathway to Paradise" first appeared in the anthology *Venturing in Southern Greece: The Vatika Odysseys* in 2006. Copyright © 2006 by Barbara J. Euser.

"Cultivating Olives" first appeared in the anthology *Venturing in Southern Greece: The Vatika Odysseys* in 2006. Copyright © 2006 by Barbara J. Euser.

"Turtle Tracks" first appeared in the anthology *Wandering in Greece: Athens, Islands and Antiquities* in 2020. Copyright © 2020 by Barbara J. Euser.

"Eternal Pavlopetri" first appeared in the anthology *Wandering in Greece: Athens, Islands and Antiquities* in 2020. Copyright © 2020 by Barbara J. Euser.

About the Author

~

Barbara J. Euser writes about gardening and travel. Her articles and essays have appeared in magazines and anthologies. She wrote *My Mediterranean Gardens, Take 'Em Along, Somaliland, Children of Dolpo,* and the children's book *The Neighbor and the Stone*. She coauthored *Golf in Greece* and *Golf in Italy*. She edited gardening anthologies *Bay Area Gardening* and *Gardening Among Friends* and travel anthologies *A Climber's Climber, Floating through France, Venturing in Southern Greece, Venturing in Ireland,* and *Venturing in Italy*. She is a retired lawyer and former political officer with the Foreign Service of the U.S. Department of State. As a director of the International Community Development Foundation, she has worked on projects in Bosnia, Somaliland, Zimbabwe, Nepal and Nicaragua.

Made in the USA
Middletown, DE
11 February 2021